BONNIE BLACKHALL

FROM QUARRIERS' VILLAGE
TO GARDEN SUBURB

Written and compiled by
Margaret McArthur

ROXBURGH PUBLICATIONS
EDINBURGH

First published in 1995
Roxburgh Publications
Tel: 0131 477 0312

Many thanks to the following for their financial sponsorship, without which the publication of this book would not have been possible.

THE BANK OF SCOTLAND

BOLAND HOLDINGS LTD.

EDINBURGH DISTRICT *arts* COUNCIL

E.H. RANSON & CO. LTD.

ROYAL BANK OF SCOTLAND.

ISBN 0 9526063 0 5

Cover Illustration: Blackhall around 1850
Painting reproduced by kind permission of the artist CHARLES BROWN

PRINTED IN GREAT BRITIAN
P. E. C. BARR PRINTERS LTD. 6 Dock Place, Edinburgh EH6 6LU

BONNIE BLACKHALL

LIST OF ILLUSTRATIONS   iv

ACKNOWLEDGEMENTS   v

CONTENTS

CHAPTER		PAGE
1	EARLY HISTORY	1
2	THE ESTATES	4
3	THE QUARRIES	18
4	THE FARMS	30
5	THE VILLAGE EXPANDS	41
6	TRANSPORT	52
7	THE BUILDING OF THE CHURCHES	62
8	SCHOOLDAYS	76
9	PEOPLE	87
10	LEISURE ACTIVITIES	95
11	THE WAR YEARS	118
12	THE GARDEN SUBURB	127
	BIBLIOGRAPHY	134
	INDEX	135

LIST OF ILLUSTRATIONS

1.	Laurie's Map of 1766	2
2.	Blackhall Village around 1865	2
3.	Blackhall 1993	3
4.	Ravelston House	4
5.	Miss Murray Gartshore	5
6.	The Overseer's House at Ravelston	7
7.	The Gardens at Ravelston	9
8.	Craigcrook Castle	10
9.	Craigcrook Estate	12
10.	The Old Lodge House at Craigcrook	13
11.	The Old Garages	14
12.	The New Office Block	15
13.	Drylaw House	16
14.	One of Ravelston's Four Quarries	19
15.	Craigie Lamb's Granddaughters about 1902	20
16.	Shepherd's Engraving of Craigleith Quarry in 1829	21
17.	An Aerial View of the Quarry Site	22
18.	Maidencraig Quarry	24
19.	Maidencraig Quarry To-day	25
20.	Craigleith Quarry when flooded	27
21.	Harvesting at Craigcrook Farm	30
22.	Ploughing at Craigcrook Farm	31
23.	Harvesting at Blackhall	33
24.	Fire at Simpson's Dairy	34
25.	" " " "	35
26.	Simpson's Dairy	36
27.	Maidencraig Garage	36
28.	Duncan's Pend	38
29.	Dean Farm	39
30.	The Garden of Maidencraig House	41
31.	Blackhall from Ravelston Woods, 1903	42
32.	Blackhall from Ravelston Woods, 1993	42
33.	Blackhall around 1920	43
34.	Queen's Avenue, half built	44
35.	Queensferry Road around 1905	46
36.	Telford Road in the 1930's	48
37.	A Bowling Club Presentation	49
38.	Blackhall in the early 40's	50
39.	'The odd SMT bus coming through Blackhall'	52
40.	Mr. Duncan with one of his horses	53
41.	A Family Outing about 1918	54
42.	'A King sellin' Codlin'	56
43.	Craigleith Station	58
44.	The Cycle Track	61
45.	St. Columba's Church	62
46.	Laying the Foundation Stone	64
47.	The Architect's Drawing of St. Columba's	65
48.	The Building of the South Transcept	69
49.	A Play in the Old Hall	71
50.	United Free Church	73
51.	The First Official School Building	77
52.	The Boarded Up School Prior to Demolition	78
53.	The Class of 1919 with Miss Aitken	79
54.	A Class in 1948	80
55.	School Huts	82
56.	Cherry Trees	83
57.	The 'New' School	84
58.	Queen's Court Retirement Houses	86
59.	Police Constable Watson	88
60.	Mr. William Scott	89
61.	Mr. George Nesbit	90
62.	The Denholm Family, 1909	92
63.	An Early Sports Day	96
64.	A Later Sports Day around 1968	97
65.	A Christmas Party in the Old Hall	97
66.	A Kinderspiel	98
67.	1990's Junior Choir	99
68.	A Scout Camp in 1934	101
69.	A Scout Presentation in 1993	103
70.	202nd Guide Reunion 1993	104
71.	Early Days of the Bowling Club	106
72.	Murray Gartshore Hall	107
73.	The First Directors of the Golf Club	109
74.	The Tennis Club	109
75.	The Blackhall Athletic Lads	110
76.	A Drama Production in 1966	112
77.	The Over-Sixties Celebrate 21st Birthday	113
78.	The Woman's Guild Celebrate 80 Years	115
79.	The Volunteers	119
80.	The Auxilliary Fire Service	122
81.	The Home Guard	123
82.	The Home Guard on Parade	124
83.	The Old Co-operative Building	127
84.	The Shops at the Corner of Groathill & Craigleith Road	129

ACKNOWLEDGEMENTS

A great many people have provided information for this book. I would like to thank in particular all the older residents of Blackhall, listed below, who have so kindly shared their memories of the area with me either directly or by sending items to the Blackhall Bulletin:-

Mr. A. Bews	Mr. R. Boyce	Miss B. Duncan
Miss E. Denholm	Miss M. Denholm	Mr. W. Denholm
Miss G. Dodds	Mrs. M Edington	Mr. H. Erskine
Mr. D. Fraser	Mrs P. Gordon	Mrs W.G. Hay
Mrs. M. Halliday	Dr. J. Harland	Miss J. Hough
Mrs M. Kerr	Miss M Lonie	Mr. A. MacDonald
Miss M. MacDonald	Mr. D. McLean	Miss M Miller
Mrs C Mittell	Mr. G. Murphy	Mr. R. Renton
Dr. A Ross	Mrs E. Stuart	Mrs. H. Sturgeon
Mrs. D. Thomas	Mr. W. Wood	Miss J. Wright.

I would like to thank them as well for providing the photographs featured in the book (apart from the modern ones).

I would also like to thank **Charles Brown** for painting the cover picture for me from the old photograph of Blackhall and thus providing the book with a colourful cover.

Thanks too, to **St. Columba's Church**, particularly **Margaret Brown**, for making their records readily available and to **Andrew Ovens** for providing information on the **Blackhall United Free Church**.

Similarly I would like to thank **Mrs. Scott** and the staff at **Blackhall School** for allowing me to browse through their records and to thank the children for their poems and views on living in Blackhall to-day. Also thanks to the **Over Sixties Club** for their Blackhall 'ditties'.

Thanks are also due to the staff of the **Edinburgh Room & Scottish Library** for all their help and to the staff at **New Register House**. I would also like to thank **Malcolm Cant** for his interest and encouragement.

And finally a very big thank you to my husband, **George**, without whose support and enthusiasm the book might never have been completed.

I little thought when I started this project five years ago that it would be such a lengthy business. It has been an enjoyable task - I hope you find it an enjoyable read.

CHAPTER 1

THE EARLY HISTORY

Historians, in the main, have recorded the lives of the rich and famous, battles, conquests and the like, but little has been written about the lives of the 'ordinary' people. The villagers of Blackhall appear to have been 'ordinary' people, indeed poor people, and have, therefore, received little or no mention in any history book.

Just how Blackhall came to be so named and when it actually came into being seems to be lost in antiquity. There are mentions of a Blackhall in early 16th century Midlothian records, but these all seem to refer to an estate near Midcalder rather than a small village 2 miles from Edinburgh.

Thus it is to Sir John Foulis of Ravelston that we are indebted for the earliest mention of this Blackhall. On 21st June, 1680 he wrote in his account book "For eall at blackhall and to John Grant when he went to Grantoune - 5s. 4d." Not much to go on but at least it shows Blackhall existed.

The next record of Blackhall is to be found in Burlaw Court Proceedings of Leith on 20th July, 1741:-

> *Complainer John Clegg upon John Craig, smith in Blackhall, for suffering six hens and a cock to feed upon complainer's rig at 10 several days preceding this day which the pursuer asserted he saw. The Court nominates John Scott in the Craig and Thomas Sheil in Groathill to visit the complainer's damage and to report and ordains to warn the defender.*

Again the information is very brief. Later records show that Groathill was a farm, do the words 'the Craig' also indicate a farm, possibly Maidencraig Farm? Perhaps the Blackhall mentioned was also a farm and that is how the village came to be so named, but it is only possible to surmise rather than state as fact. It was 1766 before Blackhall warranted a mention on a map (Laurie's - see page 2)

Blackhall did not have its own parish church until the turn of this century, which would seem to indicate that it was indeed a small village. It also had the misfortune of having the parish boundaries of three other church - St. Cuthbert's, Cramond and Corstorphine - trisecting the village. Thus Blackhall is not mentioned in Sir John Sinclair's Statistical Accounts of Scotland 1791-1799, which can normally be relied upon to give some information on an area, nor does there appear to be any early record of the village in the records of the above churches.

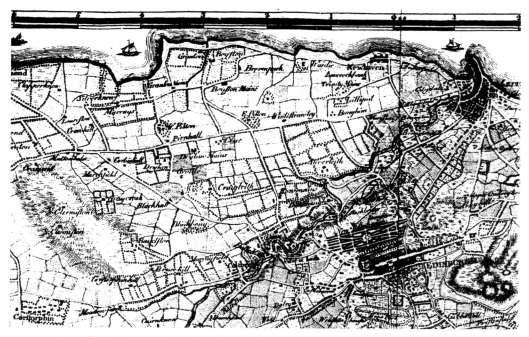

Laurie's Map 1766 Reproduced by kind permission of Edinburgh City Libraries

The first detailed information on Blackhall comes from the 1841 Census and even then, as it was taken according to Parish Boundaries, it is difficult to piece together a completely accurate picture. However, it would seem that, at that time, there were some 49 houses in the village and a further 7 in the Craigcrook estate and 9 on the Ravelston estate, housing 167 males and 146 females, making a total population of 313 in the area.

Blackhall Village around 1865

Of these people, five were listed as gentry, four as overseer/stewards, 34 as servants. Three were farmers and 33 were agricultural labourers. There was one stone merchant, three stone carriers, three wrights, eight quarriers, 13 labourers, six blacksmiths and one surveyor.

The village could also boast of three spirit merchants, one grocer, one meal merchant, one weaver, one joiner, one apprentice shoemaker, one toll keeper and one teacher.

It can be seen from the above that the villagers depended on the neighbouring estates, quarries and farms for their livelihood and, as early records have been kept on these, it is possible to get an inkling of what life was like for the villagers.

Blackhall 1993

CHAPTER 2

THE ESTATES

Blackhall was not only divided by three parish boundaries but also by three estate boundaries.

When RAVELSTON ESTATE was sold in 1915 it covered some 283 acres of the area, taking in the Bowling and Tennis Clubs, the Park, both Ravelston & Murrayfield Golf Courses, part of Corstorphine Woods as far as the 'Rest & Be Thankful', plus Marischal Place and the Keiths.

The CRAIGCROOK ESTATE also covered part of Corstorphine Woods and extended over the hill to include Clermiston Farm with March Road, Queensferry Road and part of Craigcrook Road forming the other boundaries.

The House o' Hills, Queens Avenue, and Groathills as far as Craigleith Quarry were latterly part of BARNTON ESTATE, but originally belonged to the DRYLAW ESTATE.

These estate divisions help to explain why some of the streets of Blackhall are somewhat confusingly named e.g. Craigcrook Road being called Keith Row, and Keith Terrace on one side of the road for part of the way, and Craigcrook Place, Gardens and Road on the other - the Keith side belonged to Ravelston and the Craigcrook naturally to Craigcrook. Many of the street names are related to past owners of the estates.

RAVELSTON ESTATE

Ravelston House

Much has already been written in other books on the history of Ravelston, but space necessitates that only a brief summary can be given here.

Ravelston appears to have been part of the barony of Dean until, by a charter in 1363, Sir William More of Abercorn donated "to God, the Blessed Virgin, and all the saints and a chaplain at the altar of the Blessed Virgin in the Church of St. Giles all the lands of Ravelston". The annual rent of these amounted to 6 lib.6sh.8d. in 1369.

At a later date the estate must have been further divided for in 1553 there is a "Confirmation of the Divided Lands of Ravelston."

In 1620 the estate came into the possesion of George Foulis, second son of James Foulis of Colinton. He was responsible for the building of the old Ravelston House which was destroyed by fire, but remnants of that period still remain in the form of an old doorway with the date 1622. There was also a fountain dated 1630 which was removed to Wemyss Castle in 1961.

Miss Murray Gartshore at the fountain dated 1630

George Foulis died in 1633 and was buried in Greyfriars Churchyard and his gravestone states "Master of the king's mint, baillie of the city of Edinburgh and sixteen years a councillor." George Foulis was succeeded by his son John, who kept the account book which gave us the first mention of Blackhall. In 1661 he married Margaret, daughter of Sir Archibald Primrose and was created a baronet of Nova Scotia. Sir John moved to Woodhall estate at Colinton in 1700 but Ravelston continued to be held by his descendents (now absorbed into Primrose of Dunipace) until 1726 when Sir Archibald Primrose sold it to Alexander Keith W.S. Sir Archibald was beheaded in 1746 for adherence to the Jacobite Cause.

The Keiths were a famous Scottish family, hereditory Earls Marischal of Scotland. In 1822 Alexander's son, also called Alexander was made a baronet by George IV when on a visit to Edinburgh. Sir Walter Scott was a relation of the Keiths and a frequent visitor to their home, and it is claimed that he used the gardens at Ravelston as a setting for his "Waverley" novels. Another literary relation of the Keiths and frequent visitor to Ravelston was Baroness Nairne, at that time the anonymous writer of many lovely Scottish songs - "Will ye no come back again", "The Land o' the Leal", "The Rowan Tree", and "Caller Herring" to name but a few. However, according to the Rev. Kirkwood Hewat writing in the Evening Dispatch in 1927, the two never met as she was a sympathiser of the Covenanters and felt that Scott had singled them out for derision, so she wrote in a letter "Poor Sir Walter, we did not put ourselves much in his way....."

Sir Alexander died in 1832 and was succeeded by his daughter, who married Sir William Murray of Ochtertyre in 1833. Writing in "Stones & Curiosities Of Edinburgh" in 1910, George A. Fothergill states "Somewhere about the year 1835 the old house was burnt down, and the central portion of it was entirely gutted, leaving but the north wing (which has undergone some little alteration, and has been turned into a house for the head gardener and steward, Mr. Jardine) and a tallish staircase-tower with crow stepped gables towards the south." The present house was built after the fire and in 1873 the Murray's son, Sir Patrick Keith Murray sold the estate to his uncle Colonel Murray-Gartshore.

In 1885 Miss Murray Gartshore had the Murray Gartshore Memorial Hall (of which more later) erected in memory of her father, the Colonel. This hall situated in Marischal Place served the community at different times in many different capacities - as the church, the school, the library, the savings bank, a recreational hall and at a much later date a small supermarket. Other houses built on the estate around that time were the blocks of cottages in Keith Row in 1893-94, and Marischal Place in 1896.

Miss Murray Gartshore died in 1914 and appears to have been much respected by the villagers as the following extract from the Blackhall Men's Association's unpublished Booklet of 1952 shows:-

Among the older generation Miss Murray Gartshore still receives her mood of praise for her habit of walking to church instead of taking her carriage. Among her many activities she distributed religious tracts to the quarries and to the best of her ability saw to it that the tenants of her houses in Blackhall kept certain standards of temperance and good conduct. She would not permit a public house to be opened on her property. Miss Murray Gartshore interpreting the dictates of religion, morality and public hygiene to the village, often no doubt found her task both difficult and unpopular; but because of her kindly interest in the people she is remembered with respect and affection. No one in our midst to-day has the same authority to supervise us. Modern restrictions usually have their source in some distant impersonal authority.

The estate was bought by Mrs. James Stewart-Clark who lived at Ravelston with her daughter Miss Stewart-Clark. **Mrs. Helen Sturgeon** has many memories of those days.

The Overseer's House at Ravelston

I came to Ravelston in 1916, the war was on - I was 16. My father was really the Overseer. We stayed in the house in the photograph. There were 15 of a staff in Ravelston House and my father had 8 men under him and there were two chauffeurs. The footmen in the house had a lovely brown livery - they were really smart. The butler, of course, was in the usual black tails. The chauffeurs wore a soft grey - there was a Rolls and another car as well. One worked the one day and the other worked the next day - they had a gentleman's life, they each had a car of their own. The housekeeper was in white.

My husband was a footman at Ravelston - he came there about 1919 as a second footman. He left a big, big place down in Ayrshire and the man there said to him "You're going down in the world instead of coming up, leaving a place like this'.... but Jack had made up his mind he was coming to Edinburgh. He wasn't there very long before the first footman got the sack and he was made first footman. He was there for six years and Todd the Butler was retiring and Jack decided to leave before a new butler came....and they sent into Hamilton and Inches and asked them to send out a selection of watches so that Jack could take his pick. They offered him the butler's job but he decided that he should go and he was away for quite a while. He got a good job up in Inverness and we were going to get married, but my father was very ill and I was an only girl and he thought it was a shame to take me away from my home when my father was ill and my mother in that big house. Well, my father died and, of course, it was a tied house, so my mother and I had to get out and eventually we got this flat in Saville Place. And one day this car draws up at the door and I recognised it as the Ravelston car and it transpired that the butler they had employed had been taken ill and they wanted Jack to go there as butler. So he worked for them until Mrs. Clark died in 1959.

Other local residents have varied memories of the Stewart-Clarks and the Ravelston gardens.

The park was gifted to Blackhall by courtesy of the two ladies, Mrs. James Stewart Clark and her daughter.....they both had their own chauffeur and their own Rolls and the two chauffeurs were Mr. Ross and Mr. Imery. And the ladies also had a little Rolls Royce, like a taxi, they used to go for messages in. At certain times of the year they had a garden fete at Ravelston - you got into certain rooms. Then they had a beautiful garden up there, a walled garden, I don't know what's in it now. They had quite a big staff.....opposite the entrance to Ravelston Golf Course, there were little cottages which were the gardeners' cottages. There's still a cottage at the entrance from Ravelston Dykes and one at the side and one opposite the garage there. They were all employed by the estate and they housed them all. There were beautiful big garages with glass fronts and there were the chauffeurs' houses and the gardeners' houses and I presume they are still there in a different form.

MR. W. WOOD

Willie Denholm and I ran the football team....Blackhall Athletic Lads. The interesting part about Blackhall Athletic, when we started the team first we hadn't a ground to play on and there was the hockey park which was owned by Mrs. Stewart-Clark. So Willie says 'What do you say we draw up a Committee and go and ask her if she'll let us play on that ground'. So three of us went up to see....we got in touch with Mr. Todd the butler and asked if we could have an audience with Mrs. Stewart-Clark and he said 'Certainly, she'll probably be pleased to see you.' So it was arranged that we would go up and 'Oh,' she says 'Of course, with one stipulation, it has to be Blackhall boys' - but it was all Blackhall boys, we were playing as a team. She got the field cut and did the pitch and goal posts, nets,corner flags and everything. She was very good, a very nice old lady she was, by that time she was a good age.

MR. H. ERSKINE

My mother used to have to go round getting contributions for the Blackhall Sports, either money or food, and she used to go up to Ravelston House and I occasionally walked with her. I think she was probably interviewed by the butler, I can't quite remember but she would get something there - and, of course, they loaned out the field for the Sports. I don't think at that time we saw anything of the actual garden, it was later on when they began to open it for the Queen's Nurses.....It was such a beautiful garden, I don't suppose it survives in any form now, but I do remember going up there sometimes.

MRS. C. MITTELL

The Gardens at Ravelston

Oh, that was a dream of a garden. There used to be a weather vane - a little man in the trees and his arm went with the wind....he was on the Ravelston Dykes Road side. We went every time the gardens were open - the last Sunday in July, they were open every year and there was a beautiful walk up to those trees through the gardens - absolutely gorgeous. There used to be the North Lodge next to the Scout Field but it's been taken away.

MISS J. WRIGHT

Mrs. Clark died in 1959 and bequeathed Ravelston House to the Church of Scotland to be used as an eventide home, and the gardens to Edinburgh Corporation. However, the death duties on the estate were so high that neither the Church or the Corporation felt able to accept the terms and the estate was sold to T. Boland & Co. Ltd., who then sold 35 acres of it to the Edinburgh Merchant Company for the Mary Erskine School for Girls.

CRAIGCROOK ESTATE

Craigcrook Castle

Craigcrook too has had a great deal written about its history and famous occupants and visitors, and once more a summary of the same must suffice.

The lands of Craigcrook date back to 1362 when they were owned by a family called Graham, who donated them to John de Alyncrum, a Burgess of Edinburgh. He settled the income from the lands on a Chaplaincy of St. Giles. In 1368 the rental of Craigcrook amounted to 6lib.6sh.8d per annum and eight years later the estate was let in feu farm at that rate to Patrick and John Leper. Thus it would appear that Craigcrook Farm was of much earlier origin than Craigcrook Castle.

The estate continued to change hands in this manner until 1542 when William Adamson, Burgess of Edinburgh, was assigned the estate in perpetual feu farm and heritage. This gentleman had extensive property extending from Craigleith to Cammo and including 'Grotthill', Clermiston, Southfield and part of Cramond Regis. The Castle was built around 1545 and Adamson was killed at the Battle of Pinkie in 1547. The estate continued to pass on to his son and heirs till 1656 when Robert Adamson broke up the large estate and sold it to different people.

Craigcrook again passed through several hands until it was bought by John Strachan W.S. in 1698. Little is known about this gentleman except that he became a W.S. on 5th November 1683, married Jane Moodie and died on 22nd April 1719.

However, when John Strachan died, he left the whole of the estate including North Clermiston plus his fortune (apart for small sums to his relatives) for charitable purposes - the Craigcrook Mortification Trust.

In Volume 5 of Cassell's Old & New Edinburgh we find the following information on the Trust:-

> "The regulations were that the rents should be given to poor old men and women and orphans; that the trustees should be 'two advocates, two Writers to the Signet, and the Presbytery of Edinburgh, at the sight of the Lords of Session, and any two of these members', for whose trouble one hundred merks yearly is allowed.
>
> There are also allowed to the advocates, fifty merks Scots, and to those Writers of the Signet one hundred merks; also twenty pounds annually for a Bible to one of the members of the Presbytery, beginning with the moderator and going through the rest in rotation.
>
> This deed was dated 24th September, 1712. The persons constituted trustees by it held a meeting and passed resolutions respecting several points which had not been regulated in the will. A clerk and factor, each with a yearly allowance of twenty pounds, were appointed to receive the money, pay it out, and keep the books.
>
> They resolved that no old person should be admitted under the age of sixty five, nor any orphan above the age of twelve; and that no annuity should exceed five pounds."

In 1827 in a Report to the Trustees, the factor stated that there were 120 pensioners on the Roll, and that, as well as paying the pensioners, he had to settle the minister's stipend and schoolmaster's salary, make two payments to the Faculty of Advocates and to the Society of Writers to the Signet, also pay the Moderator's officer's salary. An allowance was also being made to the gardener at Craigcrook for superintending and watching the hill to ensure that no unauthorised person shoot upon the estate. The factor received £40 for these duties. Just where the above minister and schoolteacher served is difficult to know, as neither Blackhall or Davidson's Mains appear to have had a school at that time, and it seems unlikely that the Craigcrook Estates would be paying the stipend of the ministers of the ancient churches of Cramond or Corstorphine. It is true that some large estates employed chaplains and school masters for the estate but it seems unlikely that Craigcrook would come into that category.

At present there are about 50 pensioners on the Trusts books, each receiving £300 per annum. The pensions are now given to people over 60 in necessitous circumstances and who have lived in Scotland all their lives. The income comes from the rental of Craigcrook Castle and the interest accrued from redeemed feus. But, to return to the history of the castle. At the beginning of the 19th century, the castle was leased to the eminent publisher Archibald Constable, who made great improvements to the Castle and grounds. His son Thomas was born there in 1812.

However, in 1815 the Castle, mansion house and hill pasture was leased at a annual rental of £75 17s to arguably its most notable occupant, Lord Jeffrey, who spent 35 seasons there. Francis Jeffrey (1773-1850) was an advocate by profession and became Lord Advocate and Member of Parliament for Edinburgh and was much involved in the politics of parliamentary reform. He edited the Edinburgh Review from its first appearance in1802 until 1829 and according to Lord Cockburn writing about Craigcrook "No unofficial house in Scotland has had a greater influence on literary or political opinion." And T. Hannon writing in the Weekly Scotsman

Craig Crook Castle, near Edinburgh from seat of Lord Jeffrey

Craigcrook Estate

in January 1927 notes - "The judge's round library contains photographs and prints of Sir Walter Scott, Sydney Smith, Lord Macaulay, Tennyson, Carlyle, Lord Cockburn and other literary lions, many of whom had been entertained in that very room."

John Hunter, son of Professor Hunter of St. Andrews, was the next occupant of the castle and was followed in 1874 by Robert Croall. The Croall family occupied the Castle until 1966.

Local resident, **Miss Mary Lonie**, has vivid memories of the Castle and the Croalls in those latter days.

We moved to the lodge of Craigcrook Castle in 1917, my father was the head gardener there. Of course, when we came here first there was nothing from the Park right along to the Castle, just a narrow road with the hedges on either side. There was no Strachan Road, Craigcrook Road just went from Blackhall straight to Davidson's Mains, and Craigcrook Farm was on the right. There was always the Ravelston Dykes Road, it came down to Craigcrook Road. It seems funny now, I can't really remember what it looked like.

The Croalls lived in the Castle then - they were undertakers and taxi drivers and they had a big place in Castle Terrace and another one down Leith Walk. When we went there first during the 1914-18 War, there were just the two sons staying in the house, Mr Douglas and Mr. James and their mother was in Spain, she had remarried

*and was a Mrs. Nightingale. They both worked at Castle Terrace in their father's
business. Mr. James Croall got married and he stayed over Craiglochart direction, and
Mr. Douglas, he got married and had a son who went to school at Loretto.*

The Old Lodge House at Craigcrook Castle

*The Castle itself was nice. There was a huge kitchen and scullery and there were
some bedrooms off which belonged to the servants and they also had a room which was
the servants' hall. A stone stair led up to the main apartments - it was all stone stairs
- the same up to the bedrooms too. On the first floor there was the billiard room with
a great big billiard table and they had seats all round about it in tiers. At the back also
there was a big room, the morning room, and off it was this little door which took you
into the tower and the library. Across from the morning room was the drawing room
and, of course, when we were there first, Mrs. Nightingale had it in the old style - big
drapes hanging down, all embroidered and different wee tables all over the place - oh,
the amount of stuff, you know the maids must have had a awful job cleaning it all.
But later it was turned into a ballroom with a beautiful floor and it had a big baby
grand piano and everything - it was beautiful. They were lovely big rooms and the
morning room had a sort of an alcove at the window and it looked right up the hill
over the field to the woods, and you could see where a bowling green had been, there
were just signs of it, they didn't have it then. Round the Castle itself, they had a
miniature golf course - for putting and 18 holes - they used to play quite a lot. And
they used to play tennis on the lawn at the back. Round the court and the lawn was a
huge border of herbaceous flowers.*

All the staff were resident, there was a lady's maid, a butler, a parlour maid, a house maid, a cook and a kitchen maid. I think that was the lot. They had a uniform, it was a dark red uniform that they wore in the afternoons, the maids, and it came high up to the neck and with wee gold buttons right down - it was nice.

The Old Garages

And then there were stables which became the garages - they used to have horses there before we went, and above the stables were the names of the horses and it was all in red and gold too. They must have had about half a dozen horses in that stable, it was quite a big stable.

The garden was at the back of the Castle and also at the side, it was all laid out in different shaped beds and was beautiful. Then there were the greenhouses - a vinery, one half was white grapes and the other half was black grapes. And a lovely one just full of flowers and another one with peaches and nectarines. And there was a small house in between we called it the stove, because we used to have the furnaces there for keeping the place warm and that was where my father brought on all his plants from seeds. Many a time I was asked to go up and help to prick out the seedlings, it was a monotonous job. I used to help him thin the grapes too, you had to do that at night, when the sun was off them and you had the long thin scissors to shape the bunches of grapes. There was a big vegetable garden too. There were just the two gardeners.

Of course, the war knocked things on the head and then they were growing vegetables instead of flowers. After the first World War, they had flowers in the gardens again. It was during the Second World war that they did away with the vineries and grew tomatoes instead - an awful lot of tomatoes. In fact, they used to sell them to Jamiesons in Princes Street - that was a lovely fruit shop, the real old kind with all sorts of fruit, exotic fruits and dishes in the window with various fruits flown in from all over.

The New Office Block at Craigcrook Castle

We were at the Castle for about 40 years. Mr. Croall was over ninety when he died and by that time, there was just him and his housekeeper in the house. Latterly my father and Mr. Croall were very, very friendly, I think it was because they were roughly the same age although my father was a wee bit younger.

I believe the vegetable garden has been made into a car park and they've built offices where the greenhouses were.

Other residents also have memories of those times.

Douglas Croall was the tenant at Craigcrook Castle when I was a boy. And we used to use the policies for the cows, and he and my father were very friendly. He owned a big garage in Castle Terrace.....it's the Social Service building now, but that was Croall's Garage. They were the main Rolls Royce agents for this part of Scotland and had taxi cabs - very big business, he was the elite......he was the boss, but he was a country gentleman. And at Craigcrook Castle, I can remember when I was a wee boy there was a bit at the front of the castle, facing up towards Corstophine Hill, that used to flood in the winter time and they used it as a curling rink.

MR. W. WOOD

The Church had a Garden Fete in Craigcrook Castle - that was in J. G. Matheson's time - that was the first really big function we ever had - it must have been about 1949 because I had been in hospital that year and really wasn't able to do much to help.

ANON

I remember some church function or something being held at Craigcrook Castle and the Croalls were still there - I don't know when that would be, but it was in Mr. Sim's time. Of course there were no houses along there then. I remember my father saying, you'll live to see the houses come right to where the sheep are grazing now and, of course, it's happened. There was nothing at Hillpark then except the old telephone exchange at the end of Craigcrook Road.

A.C.

We used to go to Craigcrook Castle - you were allowed to get in - you had to apply to the Craigcrook Mortification Trust - I've been once or twice in Craigcrook, it was lovely - but then somebody took it over and you can't get in now. You used to be able to walk over from the zoo, climb a wall and walk down. And when I taught at Clermiston, I used to come down through the woods and home for my lunch.
MISS J. WRIGHT

The only memory I have of the Croalls at Craigcrook was when the gallery extension was made at the church in 1935 or 36.....they were there for some reason or other.
MR. A. MACDONALD

THE DRYLAW ESTATE

Drylaw House

The Drylaw Estate is also of ancient origin with records dating back to 1406, but as Drylaw House is outwith the present Blackhall parish boundary, only a brief history will be given here. In the 15th century the estate was owned by the Forresters of Corstorphine and in the 16th by the Macgills. In 1641 it was sold to James Loch and remained with that family until bought by William Ramsay of Barnton in 1786 for £24,000. At that time the estate included the following farms Wester Drylaw (67 Scots acres), Easter Drylaw (107 Scots acres), Groathill (78 Scots acres) and Pirniehill (64 Scots acres).

An Ordnance Gazetteer of 1882 gives us the following information on Barnton:-

A mansion in Cramond parish near the River Almond 4¾ miles WNW of Edinburgh. It stands on or near the site of Cramond Regis, an ancient hunting seat of Scottish Kings; and until recently the seat of the Ramsays of Barnton, it now belongs to Sir James Ramsay-Gibson-Maitland who, born in 1848 succeeded as fourth baronet in 1876. A magnificent park of nearly 400 acres surrounds it.

Sir James' eldest daughter Mary married the Rt. Hon. Sir Arthur Steel-Maitland, who sold Drylaw House back to the Loch family.

One of the tenants of Drylaw House did, however, have close connections with Blackhall, as J. Stuart K. Milne writing in his booklet "Blackhall" in 1963 narrates:-

The local Scout Troop was founded in 1909 as the 53rd Edinburgh under Mr. A. S. Nicolls as Scoutmaster. It was joined in 1910 by Lieut. A.C. Dewar of Drylaw House, who became Scoutmaster in 1911 of the 23rd Midlothian, for thus it was then called, Blackhall being outwith the city boundary. In 1912 a small drum and bugle band was started, having its lessons at Drylaw from a Drum Major Scotland of Edinburgh Castle.

Drylaw, where the Troop met in a loft of the stables (which were the only remnant of the House destroyed by Lord Hereford in 1544) formed the venue of many a Troop function, be it tea on the lawn, lunch in "the park" (a large field still extant within the inner wall of the estate) or a patriotic gathering in the garden.

The Troop took out a lease dated 13th July, 1911 on a small stable at Simpson's dairy (Up a lane near the present Roadhouse). Not until 1913, when Lieut Dewar who had been studying at Oxford returned, did the stable loft at Drylaw again come into use as Troop Headquarters. On 11th July 1914 a Sports Day was held at Drylaw when Lieut. Dewar's mother gave the tea and Mr. James Simpson of Blackhall provided the double cream. "I never see cream like that now," remarked Capt. Dewar writing a few years later.

The outbreak of war saw the departure of both Lieut. Dewar and his assistant Bill Hogg but the Troop continued to meet. When Lieut. Dewar's mother passed away in 1915 the Troop were soon unable to continue using Drylaw as their headquarters and returned once more to the stable in Blackhall where they were permitted "to keep some of our gear in Mr. Simpson's House o' Hill Dairy loft".

Captain Dewar, possessor of the Scout Medal of Merit, did not return until 1921 and the Troop, which lost nearly half its members in the Great War, was disbanded a year later. "So the buglers of the 23rd sounding the last post of peace time at our camp in 1913 were sounding the last post of the old 23rd for me." Thus wrote Captain Dewar in 1958, when the 23rd, after a period of meeting at Craigcrook Farm and the old Recreational Hall in Blackhall was meeting in the spacious accommodation of the newly erected halls of St. Columba's Church.

THE QUARRIES

The 1841 Census showed that nearly 20% of the village men worked in the quarries, but finding out what life was like for them has proved to be difficult. In an excellent little book entitled "Building Stones of Edinburgh", (edited by A.A. McMillan and published by the Edinburgh Geographical Society), there is the following comment:-
"Most quarrymen were probably illiterate so it is hardly surprising that we have so few accounts of what it was like to work in a quarry when stone was won by human muscle."

However, there is sufficient information in that book, both on the quarriers and on the local Blackhall quarries to give a reasonably clear picture.

In the early sixteenth century during the summer months quarriers worked from 5am. to 7pm. with a two hour break at midday and two half hour breaks, one for breakfast and one in the afternoon. In winter they worked from dawn to 11.30 am and then from 1 pm till dusk. By the 18th century summer hours had been reduced to 6am. to 7pm. with one hour for breakfast and another for lunch. Most work was carried out in the summer months and the shorter winter days meant a reduction in wages for the quarriers. The amount of work was also dependent on the demand for stone for a particular building and the men often had to work different quarries in the course of a week.

In Scotland there was no great distinction made between the different types of stone workers. The work of winning stones was done by men described as workmen. Quarriers were the skilled men with whom the masters of works make the contracts to quarry specific amounts of stone. Sometimes quarriers may have moved up the social scale to become masons who were members of a trade.

It was not a healthy life. Apart from the dangers of accidental injury, there were hazards connected to working with sandstone, particularly that from Craigleith. In the 1850's a Dr. Alison noted that 'an old Craigleith man was done at 30, died at 35'. He recommended that the men should grow beards and moustaches which would act as respirators. In the same decade, the first Director of the Industrial Museum of Scotland, Dr. Wilson stated that the trouble lay in the fine irritating sandstone powder and not, as the stoneworkers believed, in the sulphur in the stone. However, it was probably healthier for the quarriers who worked in the open air than for the masons who dressed stones in sheds where much dust was created.

But what of the local quarries which were an important source of employment for the men of Blackhall?

THE RAVELSTON QUARRIES

One of Ravelston's Four Quarries

There were four main quarries on the Ravelston estate, two in the region of the Ravelston and Murrayfield Golf Clubs, one behind Blackhall Primary School near Craigcrook Castle, and another behind the field commonly known as the Scout Field, which is bounded by Ravelston Park, Ravelston Dykes Road and Craigcrook Road. These are the oldest quarries in the area and appear to date back to 1511-12. These quarries provided stones for Holyrood Palace, St. Giles Cathedral, Heriot's Hospital and Parliament House. They seem to have been inactive for a number of years but in 1845, it is recorded that the quarries had been drained and a tenant was being sought. When the first Quarry List was published in 1895, 16 men were employed by the quarries and this had fallen to only 5 in 1909. After the First World War, 28 men were taken on but activity gradually declined and the last year that Ravelston appears on the quarry list is 1939.

But there are many in Blackhall and beyond who have memories and knowledge of the quarries and the men who worked them. **Mr. W.G. Hay** of Granton Road sent the following information to the Blackhall Bulletin in 1985.

Thomas Lamb was manager of the Ravelston Estate in 1841 and supervised the two old quarries - the one near the Park and the other near Craigcrook Castle. Near the 9th and 17th greens of Murrayfield Golf Course are the disused Fountainhead and Ravelston Quarries, which were worked by Thomas Lamb's sons Craigie and Robert, and thereafter by Robert's son Thomas. These are the quarries reached by turning right just past the house on the corner of Ravelston Golf Course.

*Tom Lamb as he was called had a house in Craigcrook Road and around the
1920's was Superintendent of St. Columba's Sunday School, where he used to lead the
hymn singing with great vigour. He once stood for Town Councillor for this Ward but
was defeated by Mr. Calder the grocer, whose shop later became Buchanan and Calder.
Some of the bungalows in Craigcrook Road and at the top of Gardiner Road are Lamb
houses.*

Craigie Lamb's Granddaughters about 1902

*Mary and Elizabeth Hogg were the granddaughters of Craigie Lamb. Their
father William Hogg, a contractor, died comparatively young and their mother
eventually had a shop, grocer and baker, in Blackhall until she moved to Trinity Road
in 1906.*

Another person with knowledge of the Hogg family is **Mr. H. Erskine**

*My grandfather was called Hogg and he had eleven of a family which was quite
fashionable in those days. Anyway he had a big house and stables at Craigleith - near
the corner of what is now Groathill Avenue - and he had the franchise for taking all
the stone out of Craigleith Quarry to build the new town of Edinburgh - him and Tom
Lamb of Ravelston Quarry. Of course that's all knocked down now, it became a
caravan site.*

And the following local people recall something of the workings of the quarry

*Next to Simpson's Dairy there was a pend where Tommy Lamb from the Ravelston
Quarry had the Steam Engines which used to take out the big lumps of stones. Tommy*

Lamb built those bungalows along opposite the Park. Charlie Barnet was the foreman - I think they stopped in the late twenties.

MR. W. WOOD

In Edwardian days I lived in Craigcrook Road and horse drawn stone carts used to pass drearily to and fro all day long, loading at Lambs Quarry in Ravelston Dykes Lane.

MRS. D. THOMAS

The two old quarries that you can see from the road up to 'the Rest and Be Thankful' were known as Lamb's Quarries and there's a road that runs up to them on the right from Ravelston Dykes Road.....and the lorries for the quarry went along that road and they were working those quarries probably up to the Second World War. What happened to them after the war I don't really know. Lamb would be an old man by that time and his manager Charlie Barnet, who was a local man, well known and involved in all sorts of things in the community, well he must have been getting near retiral age by the time the war ended too.

MR. R. BOYCE

CRAIGLEITH QUARRY

Craigleith was the largest and probably the best known quarry in the area. It supplied most of the stone for the New Town of Edinburgh, but goes back to a much earlier period. It is first mentioned in 1615 (when called Innerleith or Enderleith) when quarriers were paid for producing 200 double arch stones for Edinburgh Castle.

Sometimes huge blocks of sandstone were excavated as in 1791 when stones were won for the six pillars at the main entrance of the Old College University. These

Shepherd's Engraving of Craigleith Quarry in 1829

measured 22ft in height and 3 ft 3 ins in diameter at the base and weighed nine tonnes. Sixteen horses were required to haul each pillar and it seemed doubtful as to whether the old North Bridge would stand up to each load. Probably the biggest block ever excavated measured 136 feet by 20 feet and part of it forms the architrave of the unfinished National Monument on Calton Hill. The remainder were sent by sea to Buckingham Palace.

The quarry was at its busiest during the building of the New Town. At one point the quarry was reputed to have been 360 feet deep and even after its 'hey-day' was past, it was still recorded as being 200 feet deep and covering 7 acres in 1892.

By 1905 only 25 workers were employed at the quarry and the stone was only used for rubble work and finally for glass cutting. In 1915 the quarry was put to a new use. The Lothian Chemical Company began manufacturing T.N.T there, as it was considered to be unsafe to prepare high explosives in a populated area, and the quarry was, at that time on the outskirts of the city.

An Aerial View of the Quarry Site giving some idea of how large it was originally

Quarrying began again after the war but employed very few men and all work seems to have stopped finally in 1941-42. After the Second World War, Craigleith was gradually filled in and is used by the Miller Group Ltd. and the new Sainsbury Superstore. Further plans are afoot for more retail developments on the site.

But local resident, **Mr. D. Fraser**, has rather different memories of the quarry:-

> *I lived in Craigleith Hill Row in the 1940's. Between our house and the Quarry there was nothing but a stretch of wasteground, apart from Craigleith Hill House (since demolished).*
>
> *The quarry was a wonderful place for brambles and I used to take the children on brambling expeditions. This is not as dangerous as it sounds, as the banks on the north side were not so steep.*
>
> *At that time Craigleith Hill Row was a cul-de-sac fenced off at the end, with a gap giving on to the grassy slope stretching down to Craigleith Road (or Barnton Terrace as it then was.) In suitable snow conditions which seemed to occur more often in those days, this made a fine sleigh run for the kids and I used to practise on my skis. The gap in the wall at the foot of the slope was known as the Hole in the Wall and the bus stop beside it was so named by the conductors of the 24 bus, the ancestor of the present 80 bus.*
>
> *The very top of the slope was rather steeper and inclined to be muddy, hence it's nickname "The Slippy". Many a time my wife would take our three children on a shopping expedition to the late lamented Co-op or any Blackhall shops. The youngest would be in the pram which she would manoeuvre down the Slippy, leaving the two older ones to make their own way. Coming back she might have to dump the groceries on the grass while she wangled the pram up to the pavement of the Row, returning for groceries and children. We were all much fitter in those days. The alternative way to Blackhall was a long round trip via Groathill Road South.*

MAIDENCRAIG QUARRY (LATER KNOWN AS BLACKHALL)

The Maidencraig Quarry was a small quarry and is first mentioned in 1628 as providing stone for Edinburgh Castle. It also provided stone for the North Bridge in 1771, but by the time of the publication of the first Ordinance Survey Map in 1853, the quarry was flooded and most probably abandoned.

Maidencraig Quarry may not have been big, but attached to it was a rather important building known locally as the Magazine House, but officially as 'The City of Edinburgh Gunpowder Magazine (situated at Blackhall)'. Regulations for the government and management of the same were made by the Magistrates & Town Council of Edinburgh and some of them make interesting reading:-

> *The magazine and its keeper will be under the Inspection of the Superintendent of Police. The keeper will reside in the lodge at the gate leading to the Magazine.*
>
> *It is the duty of the Keeper to wear the Magazine coat and shoes with which he is provided.*
>
> *With the exception of the Magistrates of the City, no persons shall be admitted within the walls of the Magazine (except those on lawful business there).*

All stores must be given out or taken in between sunrise and sunset.
No powder will be received or given out during a thunderstorm.
No intoxicated person will be admitted at the gate and no smoking or use of fire
of any description will be permitted within the enclosure around the Magazine.

Maidencraig Quarry – The Magazine House can be seen in the background

In the 1890's the keeper of the Magazine was a gentleman by the name of Robert
Burns from Dumfries, who created quite a stir in the Edinburgh and Glasgow
newspapers of 1895. The gentlemen of the press felt that it was unseemly that the
great grandson of Scotland's national bard should live in what they considered to be
poverty stricken circumstances and urged Burns admirers and clubs to help him out of
his difficulties. Two things thwarted their efforts. The first was that Mr. Burns could
not understand what all the fuss was about, as he considered that £52 a year plus a free
house and garden was quite a comfortable living. The second was that it transpired
that Mr. Burns was not a lawful descendant of Robert Burns. His ancestry went back
to the poet's eldest son Robert, to whom an illegimate son had been born while he was
in London. This third Robert Burns went on to keep a private school in Dumfries,
where his son Robert - the Magazine keeper - was educated. Eventually the publicity
subsided and Mr. Burns and his wife were left to enjoy the peace of their Blackhall
cottage.

Several Blackhall residents recall the Powder Magazine and the Quarry.

Along Maidencraig Crescent there was a powder magazine house, and my father used
to take the powder away to different quarries, away to Balerno and all over. There was

a Mr. Fraser, I think he'd been an army officer, he used to look after the magazine house and chase away the laddies, because it would be dangerous.

MISS B. DUNCAN

In the first World War shells and amunition were made in Craigleith Quarry and were brought round by four horses and a big double yoked lorry and taken up the lane to Maidencraig and stowed in the Magazine House. There was nobody looked after the Magazine House when we used to run around that quarry playing Cowboys and Indians. The door was open and you went in and it was all overgrown with weeds and trees, the only way you could tell it had been a magazine house was all the callibrations of the different shells that were kept in there......the army used to have a van sort of thing pulled by 4 mules and the shells were loaded on and taken away.

MR. H. ERSKINE

We used to play a game...I can't remember what it was exactly, but you tried to touch the trees on the main road, where the Roadhouse is now. Having done that, you touched the wall at the side and then you went away round to what they called the powder magazine at the back...some of the men used to sit there puffing on their pipes and would bellow at us.....

DR. J. HARLAND

Some time after 1926, the Corporation acquired the site, demolished the Magazine House and installed an incinerator. The town's refuse was brought there and reduced to ashes until eventually the quarry was filled in and levelled off.

MR. R. RENTON

Scottie went round with a horse and cart, Duncan supplied the horse and cart and the rubbish was dumped into Maidencraig Quarry and eventually they built an incinerator and they burnt all the stuff before they discharged what was left into the quarry.

MR. H. ERSKINE

The Site of Maidencraig Quarry today

THE MARL OR MARLE PITS

Although not strictly speaking quarries, the marle pits were such a landmark in the Blackhall area that it is only fitting that they should be mentioned here.

Under the Parish of Cramond in the 1791-1799 Statistical Account of Scotland, there is the following statement - "Marle was discovered some years ago on the farms of Marchfield and Craigcrook where a considerable quantity was procured: but the working is becoming very expensive, is now discontinued and the pits drowned."

The dictionary defines Marl as "being a fine grain clay, often used as manure: a soil containing carbonate of lime."

All of which ties in with local knowledge and memories.

"MacTaggart and Mickel let it out as allotments until a couple of years ago and all that ground is beautiful sandy soil and if you dig about 6 feet in, it is pure sand and there are very few stones. And all that top soil came off the hill and it all settled as a sort of bog as it were - it was beautiful soil and they called it Marle.

MR. W. WOOD

And then, of course, at the far end of March Road were the Marle Pits, which have all been filled in now - at one time there were greenhouses and allotments there.

DR. A.ROSS

However, the original drowning of the pits caused a loch to be formed which is remembered by many of our older residents and which led to Craigcrook Road being known as the Loch Road by some. It also gave rise to a legend which persists to this day.

I mind of the Marle Pits - a horse and cart went into them at one time and just disappeared - I used to go along the Craigcrook Road on my bike, before the Strachan Road was built

MRS. H. STURGEON

The Marle Pits were where the very expensive houses are being built at the end of Craigcrook Road now. I never went near that because Mrs. Hogg, who kept the fruit shop, said that a coach and pair had gone into there and so it was regarded as a totally 'keep out' area.

MISS M. MACDONALD

And, of course, there was the rumour that down March Road there was this great field that was supposed to be so wet that at one time a stage coach had got lost.....I just wonder if they ever found a stage coach when they were working there - at the Marle Pits.

MISS J. WRIGHT

We were not allowed to go anywhere near the Marle Pits, that was one place that was forbidden. They were supposed to be bottomless, that's what we were told, if you fell in you would never get out.

MISS M. DENHOLM

Possibly the legend had some basis in fact but had presumably been greatly exaggerated, possibly by parents, anxious to keep their children away from the dangers which definitely existed in both the Marle Pits and the quarries.

I remember one of the ploughmans' wives was drowned there - I don't know if it was an accident or suicide but she was found in the Marle Pits...they were treacherous.

MISS M. LONIE

We were dared to go near any of the Quarries with water in them, although my brother used to go and swim in it. Mother didn't know, she would have had kittens - that was at Stevie's Quarry the one at the back of the School - it was very dangerous, I mean there were one or two people drowned in it, because I think there were weeds and that sort of thing.

MISS E. DENHOLM

I remember I first heard about Craigleith Quarry when I was at Wardie School. The brother of a boy in my class went bird-nesting there and was drowned - it's imprinted in my head because at that age it was such a dreadful thing to happen.

MRS E. STUART

Craigleith Quarry when flooded

We used to go fishing in Stevies Quarry - Ravelston Quarry was Clarks Quarry and you could catch perch in there and eat them because that was a clean quarry. Stevie's Quarry was further along Craigcrook Road, you came to a field and went over the gate and there was a bull in that field, I used to watch for the bull away at the far end, then I'd go over the gate, go like a bat from hell across to the wall and get up before he got across to me. There were plenty of fish in Stevie's Quarry but I think it was a deep quarry.

MR. H. ERSKINE

It was a dangerous quarry - that one between the golf course and the castle garden. When friends came out to see us, we used to go through the gate into the plantation and then walk round the quarry, but it became too dangerous - there were two or three deaths when we were there. It was full of water and treacherous. I remember one time in particular, there was a boy - the boys used to come out and fish and what have you - and this boy was from Leith and he was drowned, he had fallen into the water and there were so many reeds and marsh growth at the foot, that he got caught in them.

And I remember the Police were out and they had a boat and all the rest of it and they were trying to grapple for him...oh, it was a dangerous place. I remember my mother saying that this boy's mother had come to the Lodge door and asked if she could see where it had happened. So my mother took her up to the quarry.....it was sad, he was just fifteen.

MISS M. LONIE

We used to play around in them but never in Craigleith - it was always well fenced in and it was always regarded as a bit too dangerous.

MR. A. MACDONALD

And then there was the quarry, of course, Stevie's Quarry, which some of the locals used to climb over the walls to....I've never been a swimmer but I've been in it when friends of mine were swimming...it really was a silly thing to do because it was a nasty deep place.

DR. A. ROSS

As laddies, we always used to be in the park and then we would nip over the wall to the quarry....I think it was quite dangerous. We used to go up the top and chuck boulders and sticks into it.

MR. D.J. MCLEAN

Yet despite this darker side of the quarries and the Marle Pits, the children of the area used them for all sorts of recreational activities.

Many a perch I pulled out of Maidencraig Quarry, I remember I fell in and got a leathering..... I went up to the house and my mother took one look at me... it wasn't a clean quarry...we just caught perch for the fun of catching them, we didnae eat them... I got a hiding. We used to play Cowboys and Indians there, it was a great place.

MR.H. ERSKINE

It always used to amaze me, when we were in Carfrae Road, the number of boys, and they weren't all local, who passed with fishing stuff going up to the quarries at Ravelston, I don't know if they still do but that was in the sixties and seventies.

A.C.

Marle Pits - I remember going with a friend who was a keen egg collector, which was regarded as quite a respectable occupation in those days, going there to get eggs.... clambering and wading out, sort of going from tuft to tuft and it was a marsh - well a marsh round the side and water in the middle and it was very good.... I mean there were a lot of ducks, I suppose they were mainly Mallards but one or two other species as well. You had to watch what you were doing, you would have water over your ankles if you didn't stand on the right tuft, you couldn't just wander on.

There was a stream ran from the Marle Pits right along the hollow between March Road and the Queensferry Road and through the Doos Wood and I suppose it was piped from there somewhere under the Queensferry Road, I don't know where it finished up. There's still a ditch along that way.

MR. A. MACDONALD

The Marle Pits was a place that you weren't suppose to go near...there were water hens and all sorts of water life there. I can't remember about the fish in it, but I know there used to be coots and wild ducks..... it was really mud and always wet.

MR. W. WOOD

The Marle Pits was another place where we went tadpoling. I believe that at one time there was a big pond there, right over to the Queensferry Road, but even when I was a lad it was quite a sizeable pond.

MR. D. J. MCLEAN

The Marle Pits....we used to go along there to look for tadpoles and sometimes it froze over in the winter time and we used to go and slide.....

MRS. C. MITTELL

I remember when we first came to Blackhall, my father used to shoot duck. Then, of course, there was the Marle Pits further down, which used to freeze over in the winter, and some folk used to skate there, but we never skated there, we used to go there for catkins, but it's funny to think of that bit all built over.

A.C.

I remember going to the quarry...Craigcrook Quarry I think it would be.....and I remember actually skating on a quarry in the winter time.

MISS M. MACDONALD

I remember sliding and skating on the quarry at the back of the school - I suppose we were tresspassing because we used to climb through the fence and cross the field to get to it - I suppose it was a bit dangerous, skating on it.
There's certainly a few of my golf balls in it now - the golf course runs along the top of it.

MR. A. MACDONALD

We played Cowboys and Indians and all sorts of things up there .....the quarry was like a basin and latterly like a Cleansing Department Dump, they had an incinerator up there... and all the rest of it, but there used to be a path that went round the top, like round the rim of the basin and you looked down on the back gardens of Maidencraig Crescent.

MR. R. BOYCE

And then we played up the Quarry, Maidencraig, and we used to build huts and have gangs and that sort of thing and it was great... there were great places to play when we were young.

MISS E. DENHOLM

The farms were also considered by the children as great places to play as you will see from the following chapter.

CHAPTER 4

THE FARMS

Harvesting at Craigcrook
The Farm buildings can just be seen in the background

According to the 1841 Census, more than a quarter of the adult population of the Blackhall area were involved in agriculture in one form or another. By 1891 this figure had gone up to 27% but by that time dairy farming had increased in importance. Now that Blackhall is a sprawling suburb, it is difficult to realise that it is just over fifty years since the last of the farms disappeared from Blackhall, but there are many living in the area who can still recall what it was like 'to live in the country'.

CRAIGCROOK FARM

As already mentioned Craigcrook Farm was of very ancient origin and covered much of the Blackhall area. According to the factor's report in 1827, the farm was occupied at that time by a Mr. Bishop, who paid a rental of £339 10s. twice a year. The farm had 19 acres of wheat, 20 acres in grass, 24 acres to be ploughed for oats, and 50 acres were to be ploughed for barley and green crops.

But it is later tenants that the older residents recall.

Craigcrook farm belonged to Mr. David Gunn, a "gentleman farmer" who bred pigs which won prizes at shows. The farm was the last word in cleanliness - and a delight to play in! Sometimes you met a large pig rooting about free-range and then you scuttled up a ladder to the top of a haystack to be out of its way. It was an arable farm and Mr. Gunn had four splendid Shire horses and a chestnut pony with a short mane like a brush called Beauty. She would be bridled and brought out for us to have rides on her back, then we might have the treat of a ride in the trap with Miss Gunn. The farm provided the haycarts for the annual Sunday School Picnic.

The ploughing season was long and tiring taking days to finish a field with a plough cutting a single furrow at a time. But the harvesting was bright and lively with the horse drawn machines reaping and binding, leaving the sheaves ready to stook. As the harvester went round and round the field and the area of corn became less, rabbits began to run for cover, but a man had a gun at the ready.

The farm with its walled secluded garden seems to me now to have been "out of this world".

MRS. D. THOMAS
(Blackhall Bulletin 1981)

The rectangle formed by Gardiner Road, Jeffrey Avenue and Columba Road in the 1920's presented an aspect very different from how it appears to-day. Gardiner Road was made up as far as the end of the terraced villas, after which it was known as "the Grass Road". Fences marked the road that was to be, but only a narrow path through the grass led to Jeffrey Avenue, which was in the same condition. Columba Road ended at a fence just past the big house called Rosenlaui. Everything beyond that was Gunn's Farm and the field between Gardiner Road and Columba Road was part of the farm. Between Gardiner Road and Craigcrook Road were the allotments. The following photograph shows ploughing taking place with the fences marking the future Jeffrey Avenue in the background and in the right hand corner the buildings of Gunn's Farm can just be made out.

MR. D. FRASER
(Blackhall Bulletin 1983)

Ploughing at Craigcrook

From our back garden we looked right up to Craigcrook Farm - Gunn's it was then and the Forests came later. Mr. Gunn wasn't very popular with my family..... before I was born they had a very nice fox terrier dog called Tip and the dog apparently died of poisoning and rightly or wrongly, Mr. Gunn was given the blame for that. And there was the feeling that he was always watching in case people did go into his fields and things like that. His fields stretched along to near where the old pond was, to where the Marle Pits were at the foot of what's now March Road. When we went to live in 22 Hillview we looked right across to the farm cottages and the road up to Craigcrook Farm by the cottages is now more or less the line of Columba Avenue. That all changed while we were still living in Hillview, they started building Columba Avenue.

MRS. C. MITTELL

I don't remember Craigcrook Farm as Gunn's Farm but knew it as Forrest's Farm from about 1926 onwards. However the entrance to the farm was on line with Columba Avenue along a narrow farm track. On the right hand side of the entrance stood an L shaped block of farm workers cottages probably about six in number, built on an elevated platform above the farm track and protected by a wall with at least two openings to give access to the cottages.

MR. R. BOYCE

In 1916 Blackhall only went as far as those stone villas on the right hand side which I think were built about 1900 and the left hand side was the same again up to Columba Road and then there were fields.

MR. W. WOOD

Forrest's Farm I knew quite well because I was friendly with the boy, Russell Forrest, who was about ages with me and went through Davidson's Mains Scouts with me. I've stooked wheat or corn or something anyway in the fields where all the Carfraes are now - Carfrae Gardens, along that ridge. I remember Columba Road came round and it was a dead-end at where Columba Avenue is now - that was the farm road and Columba Road finished there and the farm house was just beyond that. Latterly they went into pigs, it was a piggery rather than arable. Of course, once they started building in Strachan Road, they had no fields left and they went into pigs and then they moved out to somewhere near Ratho. I think it was well into the thirties before it finally went, because I remember these farm cottages being there well on. I was probably working by the time they disappeared.

MR. A. MACDONALD

When we came to Gardiner Road in 1929 there were no houses opposite, there was just the big farm shed. And when the farm was there, Mr. Little next door, he had just got his garden sort of laid out and one morning when he came through, the pigs had come over from the farm and dug or burrowed into his ground with their noses, the way pigs do, and he had to start all over again. Gardiner Road was quite a rough road then and there were no shops at the top at all. They were cutting corn beyond our back garden - it was all fields, Strachan Road wasn't there and there was a farm road from the next block right through down to the low road - Craigcrook Road - it was a great walk for people with their dogs. It was more a farming community really here because we got off the bus in the village and we had all this rough road to walk up and there were no lights at that time.....really rural then, I've seen a big change.

ANON

Harvesting at Blackhall

I used to play in Craigcrook Farm, it was empty at that time..... lovely garden it had, we certainly played up there and at the wee farm cottages at the end of the road.

MISS M. DENHOLM

Craigcrook Farm - my mother's house was built in 1935 and I reckon the farm would be down before 1940 because then the houses were built across the road from us.

MR. D.J. MCLEAN

I don't remember very much about Craigcrook Farm. I remember the cottages up there - I think some of the people from there came down to live where...what we used to call the Happy Valley, that's the houses next to the Roadhouse, these four flats. Well, there were eight flats then and I think when they demolished the cottages some of them came to live there. I don't remember the farm, but I do remember when they were building houses up there because we used to go and play in them and that must have been before the war.

MISS E. DENHOLM

But there were occasions when the farms caused great excitement in the village.

There was a period in the late twenties and early thirties when, on various occasions, fires occurred at the farm and this caused great excitement in the village as the Fire Engines of the time raced through Blackhall with bells clanging - needless to say the fires attracted many spectators.

MR. R. BOYCE

I remember an occasion when the hayricks at Forrest's farm had gone on fire - my father must have seen it or heard about it - and we all paraded up to the farm to watch.

MISS M. MACDONALD

The first year we were here (1929), there was a big fire in the hay stacks - it was quite a blaze we had to shut all our windows and doors and the mice were running across the street - it was terrible.

ANON

One year the hay ricks went on fire. That was a great night for us - I don't know what it was for the Forests - the fire brigade were still there when we left about 10 o'clock at night..... there were about twenty stacks and they all went - I don't remember any buildings going, I think it was confined to the stacks.

MR. A. MACDONALD

There does not appear to be any photographs of the fire at Craigcrook Farm, but a fire at Simpson's Dairy around the turn of the century also caused a stir.

This photograph has been taken from half way along Keith Row looking towards the Queensferry Road, The Craigcrook Place flats had not yet been built

Simpson's Dairy was a lovely building - and I can remember he had a place at the back that was all tiled where he did the cream - it was beautiful, a beautiful building.

MR. W. WOOD

J.C. Simpson - he was quite a character, he was an elder in the kirk and he did all sorts of things - very well known in the neighbourhood. It was a beautiful dairy, I was sent down with a pitcher to get milk and there was no measure, they just filled up your pitcher and you paid your money and you went away, just like that.

DR. J. HARLAND

Blackhall Dairies - there was McAnsh which was just a shop where the dry-cleaners are now. And then there was Simpson's Dairy somewhere about where the Royal Bank and the Savings Bank are now on the other side. We always got our milk from McAnsh because they were on our side of the street but a friend of mine who lived down the foot of Queen's Avenue, they dealt with Simpson and I often went round with him. You went round with your metal churn and got a pint of milk that way and I always remember going in there and seeing these great flat galvanised saucer things they were using for letting the cream come to the top and presumably it was skimmed off to sell as cream. And you used to meet the cows from Simpson's coming back along Craigcrook Road, they grazed I think if I remember rightly in the fields that used to be between Corstorphine Woods and Craigcrook Road, what is now Hillpark.... the cows grazed there and they were brought along at night to be milked.

DR. A. ROSS

This photograph is from the corner of Marischal Place

When we were wee we used to play in the dairy, Simpson's Dairy, and we had a great time there until we were chased out by somebody. But on a Friday, I think it was a Friday, McVities used to send their broken biscuits - they were soft biscuits - for the cows, but we were always over first to see if we could get the biscuits first....all the kids in the village went round then.

MISS E. DENHOLM

I remember calves at Simpson's Dairy, they were just off the road..... there was a sort of pend there and you went in and there was a house on the left and then there were the cows and the calves.

MISS M. MILLER

We got our milk at Simpson's Dairy when we first came out to Blackhall. It was a popular place to go, when my mother went to pay the account, we always went with her and we were given a penny.

MISS A. MACDONALD

When I was a small boy I used to drive the cows to the grazing fields from Simpson's Dairy and then brought them back again later for milking. On many occasions too I helped to drive the cattle to market at Gorgie via Ravelston Golf Course and Ravelston Dykes. The dairy was in the centre of the village and many a happy hour I spent 'helping' and playing in the farmyard.

MR. G. MURPHY
(Blackhall Bulletin 1981)

A clearer view of Simpson's Dairy

Pryde's Dairy was where the fish shop used to be, McAnsh's Dairy was where the dry-cleaners are now…. their ice cream wasn't as creamy as the Pryde's one, that was the one we used to get, a ha'penny ice cream. This was after Simpson's Dairy, of course.

MRS. M. EDINGTON

The McAnsh family all helped at the dairy where huge containers of milk stood on a marble slab and a long-handled scoop was used to fill the customers' pitchers. Milk was also delivered to the house in a metal pitcher with a close fitting lid, and if cream was ordered, a similar small pitcher was hooked on the handle of the large one

MR. B. FRASER
(Blackhall Bulletin 1983)

MAIDENCRAIG FARM

Maidencraig Garage

Some of the old buildings of Maidencraig Farm can still be seen as part of the garage of the same name in Queensferry Road. Three generations of Woods have lived at Maidencraig Farm/Villa/Garage and **Mr. William Wood Senior**, now retired from the garage, recalls the time when it was a farm.

I was born in Davidson's Mains in a farm called Peggy's Place - that's part of Corbiehill Road now. It was a dairy farm, the difference between dairy farms and agricultural farms, the dairy farms in those days, the cows were kept indoors and they were fed on by-products of breweries, what they called draught and molasses which came in barrels, and hay and swede turnips - that was the winter feed and they were put out in the fields in the summer and brought back twice a day for milking. We moved to Blackhall in 1916, Maidencraig was a Dairy Farm too - and we used to use the policies at Craigcrook Castle and the cows were driven along there in the summer time. We kept pigs later on. Work started about four or five in the morning, the cows had to be fed and mucked out or in the summer time taken along to the fields. We used to have to drive them along to the cattle markets when we were selling...along Craigcrook Road and up Ravelston and down Murrayfield Road and I can remember that quite often they used to get into the gardens at the side and make such a mess, trampling rose bushes......

I remember when I was young, where Maidencraig Crescent is, that was a field right over to the old Blackhall School, very steep, parallel with the old quarry wall and it went over to the railway, that was one of the fields that was used for turnips and all sorts of things.

There was no Telford Road in those days - there was the Ferry Road and the Queensferry Road and there was a little road which connected with the Queensferry Road at Craigleith. There was a rhubarb field at the corner and there was the quarry on the other side. Then there was the railway goods yards, where they later sold the caravans - my father used to buy cattle in Skipton in Yorkshire and they came up on the train and were unloaded there and it was surprising how quickly they came and in perfect condition.

It was about 1937 that my father changed it to a garage. Circumstances had changed, more people were coming to live in the area because the city was growing. You found that your way of life - you couldn't do things the way you were use to - where there's animals there's smells and you get people complaining and the public health saying "Oh, you've to do this and you have to do that" and you get to the stage where it is impossible to keep going. It's just one of those things, like everything else....you've got to move with the times or get out.

Others too have memories of Maidencraig as a farm.

Every year in front of the dairy buildings, he used to have calves out there and they were a great attraction for the kids - to see the calves. But they used to drive the cattle up Craigcrook Place and along Loch Road - Craigcrook Road was the Loch Road - it made you realise that you were in a country village.

MR. R. BOYCE

Maidencraig was a Dairy and it was McCormack that was in it before Wood. There used to be a cottage at the front of the dairy, and they knocked it down when they made the car park bit of the garage - I lived in that cottage for a bit. It was quite big with five or six rooms. The Woods took over after McCormack died. After we left the cottage Murray the Coalmerchant took it over

MISS B. DUNCAN

And the Woods were at Maidencraig and Mrs. Wood used to come out and meet the cashier and one of the counterhands from Davidson's Mains Store. They came off the train there and walked to Davidson's Mains in those days, and Mrs. Wood used to come out with her book and her cheque and her order and at Christmas time she always gave them a bottle of perfume.

MRS. H. STURGEON

There were also other farms in the area which gave work to the Blackhall villagers.

Tom Duncan had his stables in the pend next to McAndrews. He had bucket type farm carts - a square sort of thing with sloping sides and front and long shafts to the horse and a man sitting up on top. They used to regularly come down of an evening, you'd see a procession of them coming down the road from the vicinity of Craigcrook Farm or beyond. He wasn't only working his horses for the farm, but he was working them for other farms around too. Beyond Craigcrook Farm you had BAIRD'S FARM, which was where you turn into Corbiehill Road and then you turn left. Then there was HOUSE O' HILL FARM....the farmhouse stood up on that high piece of ground at House o' Hill Brae, it was quite majestic sitting on a grassy hill up there - a big farm house, and of course there were no bungalows around.....the next building you came to was Davidson Mains School.

MR. R. BOYCE

The entrance to the pend can be seen on the left

In 1891 the Scotsman carried an advertisement regarding a replenishing sale at
HOUSE O' HILL FARM and EAST PILTON FARM. Listed in the sale were 10 work
horses, 1 harness horse, 70 head of poultry; 6 stacks wheat, 15 stacks oats at House o'
Hill; 10 Close carts, 5 long carts, water barrel on wheels, 2 drill sowing machines plus
numerous other machine. Also mentioned in the advertisement, were one grieve and
four ploughmen for House o' Hill and a grieve and two ploughmen, a quarterman and
a groom for East Pilton. Whether the House o' Hill Farm turned to pig farming after
that sale or at a later date is difficult to know, but it is remembered as a pig farm by
local residents.

*And another favourite walk when I was small was up to Davidson's Mains where there
was the piggery and I remember being greatly thrilled one day to hear the man calling
one of the pigs Willie.....I had never thought of them having names. That was up at
the House o' Hill area, it probably was House O' Hill Farm. It's all built up now.*

MISS M. MACDONALD

At the other end of the village, there was GROATHILL FARM at the present
junction of Groathill Road South and Telford Road. This farm was also of ancient
origin dating back to the 14th century and became part of the Drylaw Estate in 1683.

*Groathill Road North was just hedgerows and it was half the width that it is now - a
country lane. There was Groathill House and Proctor's Farm at the bottom - it was to
the left of the Doocot. I think the doocot is still there. Mr. Proctor he was a prominent
member of Blackhall Bowling Club - a handsome man he was and he had this big
farm house down at Drylaw and, of course, his farm was quite extensive too.*

MR. R. BOYCE

*There used to be a row of cottages where the Caravan Park is now. I remember when
I was at Blackhall School, there were children came from these cottages - they probably
belonged to Groathill Farm.*

MISS M. DENHOLM.

Another Farm at that end of the village was the DEAN FARM

Dean Farm photographed from Ravelston Dykes

Dean Farm - it was Stewart's Farm. I used to deliver papers there in the morning. The farmhouse stood where the Esso Garage is now. The courtyard of the garage was shrubs, and they had two gates, and it was a crescent shaped drive, you went in one end and the house stood in the middle, a great impressive mansion house, and you came out at the other. The fields for Stewart's Farm stretched right up to Ravelston and towards the town as far as Queensferry Terrace.

MR. R. BOYCE

Stewart's Farm was over where the Esso Garage is now. They used to bring the sheep from the Gorgie Market and put them in the fields there.

MRS. H. STURGEON

The Dean Farm was all fields - all that ground where the bungalows and newer houses are, I'm talking about the ones built after the first World War, that was all fields. I went to Daniel Stewarts and we walked to school and it was fields all the way, there was nothing - no bungalows or anything like that.

MR. W. WOOD

Edinburgh continued to grow and spread, and indeed continues to grow and spread, but it was several decades before the village was completely swallowed up by the city.

CHAPTER 5

THE VILLAGE EXPANDS

By the 1891 census, there were signs that Blackhall was expanding but not very rapidly. The number of houses in the area had increased to 82 and the population to 375. The gentry had reduced to three but there were still some 33 servants, there were only two farmers but some 49 agricultural labourers (many of whom were employed in dairies). There were 15 quarriers and 15 labourers but only two blacksmiths. But the greatest sign of expansion was that the village now had seven working in the grocers/wine merchants trade, had acquired a post office which employed three and warranted a village policeman. The opening of the Granton Branch Line by Caledonian Railways in 1861 for goods and 1879 for passengers meant there were also ten railway workers living in the village.

Later censuses are not available for perusal because of the 100 years confidentiality act, but the Registrar General gives the following figures for Blackhall:-

    1901 - 165 houses with a further 16 being built - population 591

    1911 - 330 houses with a further 5 being built - population - 1,474.

From the above figures, it can be seen that there was only a small increase in the population between 1841 and 1891 but a significant increase between 1891 and 1901 followed by a further doubling of the number of houses by 1911. Comparison of ordinance survey maps also gives some idea of the rapid expansion.

However, there were signs of progress even before this date. Sometime between 1861 and 1871, Blackhall acquired an Inn, which also housed the Postmaster. Just exactly where it was situated is quite difficult to tell as names of buildings seemed to change from one census to the next. However, it appears to have been in the Maidencraig area for in the 1891 Census, it appears between the Magazine House and Maidencraig House (not Maidencraig Villa which was listed elsewhere in the census).

Maidencraig

The Garden of Maidencraig House is on the left.

House was replaced by the House o' Hill Pub, now the head office of Capital Foods, and is remembered by some of Blackhall's ex-residents

I came to Blackhall when I was 6 and stayed in 7 Marischal Place, that's now a shop. Then we shifted from there to Maidencraig House, which was my mother's property, so when my mother died we shifted out of there, my mother died in thirty four. It was sold to White the Builder and he built the House o' Hill Pub.

MR. H. ERSKINE

I remember the house that was there before the Roadhouse. Sort of set back from the road, I always thought it was a forbidding sort of place. It had a garden in front with mature trees all round it and there was a path with a few steps up to the door which was central in this biggish house - it had two stories.

MISS M. MILLER

Blackhall Inn was sold to a Barbara Ross in 1896 and in the Register of Sasines it was stated as being:-

24 poles of ground, north side of the High Road from Edinburgh to Queensferry near the West End of the village of Blackhall and bounded on the east by a narrow lane or close with the dwelling house and offices sometimes called Blackhall Inn, being part of the lands of Maidencraig in the parish of St. Cuthbert's.

Above – Blackhall from Ravelston Woods, 1903, The 'Iron Church can be seen in the distance, the present St. Columba's is in the process of being built. **Below** – The same view 1993

Other signs of expansion were the building of a Recreational Hall in the village in 1885 by the Murray Gartshores of Ravelston, and in 1898 the Kirk Session of Cramond Kirk deciding that Blackhall was now large enough to have its own church building and raising the necessary funds for the same. Around 1906 Cramond School Board decided that Blackhall also required a school building as the children were at that time meeting in the Recreational Hall.

In 1911 firm proposals were being put forward to turn Blackhall into a 'Garden Suburb'.

The children of some of these early 'settlers' recall what the village was like.

> *I was born in the last house in Craigcrook Road at that time - it was called the Linden then, I think it has a number now, 24. I was born in 1914, my parents had come out from Comely Bank. Jeffrey Avenue at that time was just a lane, a grass lane, and there was broken paling across the end of it and we used to turn somersaults on it. There was a track that just led up to Columba Road and the church. Behind Craigcrook Place and Road right along to Jeffrey Avenue, there were allotments.*

MRS. C. MITTELL

Aerial View of Blackhall around 1920, the allotments are clearly visible and the school can just be seen in the top right hand corner.

> *I was born in Blackhall at 2 Gardiner Road and at that time there were only two houses in Gardiner Road - Nos 2 & 4. Later the made-up part of Gardiner Road stopped at the end of the row of terraced houses and then there was what we used to call the grass road - there were the fences and the grass growing and a little path through it along to Jefffrey Avenue which was the same and then you turned left and went down to Craigcrook Road and there was a fence across the bottom of the road there with just a gap in the fence to get through it. Craigcrook Road wasn't built any*

further along than the park. Columba Road just went up so far, just round the corner, then there was a fence across and it was Gunn's fields beyond that. Craigleith Road was called Barnton Terrace at that time and there were no bungalows then just fields. There was a farm - Groathill/Drylaw - I think the Doocot still stand among the houses. There must have been a pond at the corner where the Doocot stands because the great thing used to be when we were young in the winter....'Drylaw's bearing' the word went round and you got your skates and went down and skated on the pond down there. And I remember in winter time sledging down Queensferry Road.

MR. D. FRASER

The old cottage that was beside the Garage was called Cragend. The last person that had it was a Miss Fleming, her father was the Butler to Lord Trainer, you know the house along at Daniel Stewarts College which is now the Boarding House, that was Lord Trainer's, he was a Law Lord. When she died, it lay empty for a long time and it was becoming dangerous and I bought it and eventually we had to knock it down.

MR. W. WOOD

I was brought, newly born, to Queens Avenue in 1920 and I was there until 1927 when we moved into Columba Road. We were the first bungalow built after Dr. Davidson's House, you know the big house...there was only Lindsay's house, which is now the Abbeyfield and the Davidson's and we were the first bungalow. There was nothing else in Columba Road until you got to the flat bit at the top where Columba Avenue is and that was the road to Craigcrook Farm - you couldn't get through beyond that because it was blocked off.
We used to go to the shops up there which had started to develop by this time.

DR. A. ROSS

I remember we had to pay feu-duty to the Steel Maitlands. All the time we lived in Queen's Avenue we had privet hedges and the story was that the Steel Maitlands had insisted that there be privet hedges planted when the houses were built. Then I think

Queens Avenue, Half built

about the end of the war, somebody had looked at title deeds and discovered that there was nothing in them that said you had to have a privet hedge - a privet hedge used to be an awful lot of work.

MISS M. MACDONALD

I was born in Seaforth Drive but it was called Hillview Terrace in these days, it was changed because there's a Hillview Terrace in Corstorphine and they decided there shouldn't be one in Blackhall. I was brought to Hillview Terrace newly born, my father did the removal while my mother was having me in the nursing home and that house was built for them along with the next door one, the semi detached houses, that's the ones in the middle of Seaforth Drive, numbers 9 and 11. That was in 1929. There was an open space opposite us that we called the Rubby Dump and we played there as children. I remember doing things like burying dead birds in a cigarette box, a Gold Flake hundred cigarette box that my father had. We lived there till 1937 then went up to Craigleith where we are now, so I think the Rubbish Dump bit was vacant until Post War.

MRS. M. EDINGTON

My grandfather came out to Craigcrook Gardens from the town and when he died, my grandmother moved into Marischal Place - there were three sons staying there with her plus a daughter and four grand children. How they coped I don't know.

My father went to live in 17 Hillview Terrace when he married in 1922 - the four terraced houses at the end. He was the first occupant. I remember we used to play in the sites of the houses being built further along. We used to play ice cream shops, I don't know if it was lime or something like that, but there were big chunks of white stuff that the workmen left and we used to cut it up and pretend to sell it to one another as ice cream. We used to run over the batons that supported the floor and try not to fall down between them and that sort of thing. And there was the bit called the dump where people used to take their garden rubbish. It was quite useful. It was on two levels and I can remember jumping down there and we had tug o' wars and all that nonsense. It was a sort of focal point to play - there were lots of kids.

MISS M. MILLER.

All the building that was going on made a grand playground. I remember playing mainly in the bungalows in Forthview Terrace because they were nearly on our doorstep and all the bungalows around Drylaw Crescent and all round there. And the houses up the Telford Road and all the Strachan Road and the Carfraes.

MR. A. MACDONALD

Roads too are remembered as great playgrounds with the lack of traffic a definite feature

When I was young, you could practically lie down in the middle of Queensferry Road and nothing would happen to you. We used to sledge there. We used to take the sledge to that opening opposite the church and the sledge started from there, right down the main Queensferry Road and we used to try to get almost up as far as Maidencraig Farm. You certainly couldn't do that nowadays, it's hard enough just to get across the road.

DR. J. HARLAND

Queensferry Road around 1905

When we were children we used to play rounders on the Queensferry Road quite safely. You got the odd S.M.T. bus but there were very, very few. And they didn't come rushing down the road, they just stopped. I think the stop was at Simpsons Dairy.

MR. W. WOOD

I can remember going out on our bikes and we tore all round the roads here and I remember racing round Columba Road and shooting out on to the Queensferry Road and down there and round what was Hillview Terrace then and you never thought anything of it. There was never enough traffic to worry us.

MR. A. MACDONALD

And I remember playing on Telford Road and bicycling on Telford Road, I mean it's unbelievable now when you think about it. There were fields on the other side of Telford Road. If you went along Forthview Terrace, at the end on the right hand side there was a big grassy patch there and we used to play on it with skipping ropes and that.

MISS M. MACDONALD

But I can remember playing as a boy on my bicycle in the building of Telford Road. There was very keen lot of young boys with bicycles and we used to play bicycle hockey in the street - I can't remember what we used, I think it must have been golf clubs and there were quite a few interesting little smashes when we were both going into the gutter to get the ball but from opposite directions.

MR. A. ROSS

Nowadays some people will wonder how Ravelston Dykes got its name, but when I was young it was a narrow road with high dykes on either side. Craigleith Road was also a narrow road and was called Barnton Terrace and West Barnton Terrace on one side and on the other side had a high wall which stretch from the corner of Orchard Brae to the junction of Queensferry Road. At the corner of Orchard Brae there was a thatched cottage which I was told had been a cat and dog home. The junction of Queensferry Road and Corbiehill Road was called Puggy's Turn but how it got that name I could never find out. The woods on the corner of Strachan Road were called Doos Woods but I can't ever remember seeing doos there, but wild strawberries used to grow there.

MR. R. RENTON

Ravelston Dykes was a very sedate place, I used to go regularly - you didn't run wild on a Sunday the way they do now, you used to go out for a sedate walk with Mum and Dad on a Sunday and often we would go up Ravelston Dykes Road, along the Dykes down Queensferry Terrace and back along the Queensferry Road to Blackhall. When I think about it now, it was really quite delightful, so peaceful and quiet.

Mind you, I'm talking about the twenties and thirties, when there were few cars, but now it's a diversion for everybody that wants to miss the Queensferry Road and it's just one car after the other tumbling down there.

MR. R. BOYCE

And some of the roads which seem very permanent features to-day, did not even exist then.

I think Strachan Road was built not long after we came out here (1924), well, maybe a few years. The top end of it was built, I remember the bottom end being built - that bottom part used to flood, I remember the house at the corner at the far side being half built and standing in ground flooded with water after rain

MR. A. MACDONALD

My father was involved in the building of Telford Road, he drove for the Carmichaels, A.M. Carmichael - my father drove all the stuff to it and also he drove to all the houses up past the kirk, that was Millers..... and that block of flats above the Banks, Sandy Forbes built them and my father drove to that. There were no other contractors in the area except away in the town. And he drove stuff to the golf courses.

MISS B. DUNCAN

I remember when the Telford Road was being built and blasted out....what I do remember is a stone, not a particularly big stone, but it came through a back bedroom window of our house at Hillview while they were blasting for the Telford Road and I think my grandmother was actually in the bedroom at the time but no-one was hurt, but I remember the window being broken.

MRS. C. MITTELL

I remember Telford Road being built. My outstanding memory of Telford Road is that when it was only half completed down to the first bridge, the road stopped and you just went straight down a rough bank and the railway was running past you there although it was fenced. Then you looked straight across to the Northern General Hospital - the Ferry Road was just a little country road, narrow without lights or houses. And I remember going down there to see an eclipse of the sun through smoked glass. I was quite young at the time and I thought this was marvelllous seeing an eclipse of the sun - we're talking about 60 or 65 years ago. It was Ian Carmichael, one of the contractors building that section of the Glasgow Road - it was called the Glasgow Road at that time, because it started all the way from Glasgow right through and this was the last leg... into Edinburgh and access to Leith Docks.

MR.R. BOYCE

I remember the Telford Road being built, we were present when they cut the first sod along at the end of Forthview Terrace, where the road juncion is now, it must have been somewhere in the middle of that - I can't remember who did it, I just remember us all going and watching this man digging up a divot. That was another useful playground - you know, when I think about what we did, talk about vandals nowadays - I can remember they had these steam shovels digging out the road, particularly that bank, the first bit of it where the houses are up on a bank, and on the Friday night I suppose it was, they used to bank the fires up on those things to keep them smouldering away until Monday morning and occasionally we used to go down and stir them up to get them burning so that no doubt by Monday morning they would be stone cold. They also had little motor boggies - a line of boggies carrying earth up driven by these little motor things and we used to start them up on the Saturdays and drive them down the line. I don't think we ever did any real damage.

MR. A. MACDONALD

Telford Road in the 1930's

As well as houses and roads being built there were other signs of expansion in the village. In 1898 The Blackhall Bowling Club was founded, and ten years later a Recreational Association was formed. Ravelston Golf Club came into being in 1912 to be followed by Blackhall Tennis Club in 1915.

The village was changing in character very rapidly, but the transition from quarriers' village to garden suburb was not completely problem free. How the adults reacted is difficult to know, but the children found there were certain divisions. Some of the children, returning from fee-paying schools in town via Craigleith Station, sometimes had to take evasive action from the occasional dry cow pats thrown in their direction when passing through the village. Occasionally the aid of a 'higher authority' was sought but, in the main, a 'separation' policy was maintained although there was an appreciation of the cause of the differences.

A large turnout of villagers at the Bowling Club's presentation of cups and medals

Some of the boys in the village school were rather rough and they delighted in giving you a cuff in the back of the neck and, of course, we were just wee boys at the time and my father went down and said 'Any more of that and I'll give you some of that'. So that was the end of that.

DR. J. HARLAND

I had very little contact with the children that went to Blackhall School. We used to talk about the village boys as if they were...... there was a lot of snobbery about then.
MR. D. FRASER

Kids being kids, we used to fight with the village children.
They would come home from school or we would come home from school....they would play football and we would shout names at one another. Now these children in

our eyes were poor because they weren't well dressed and yet we all went to Sunday School and some of them were in my class and I was quite friendly. It's strange really because my father lived in Marischal Place and it was only once these peripheral houses were built that the poorer people were left behind. The village children lived in Marischal Place and the houses opposite.

I went to Miss Mather's little school and I used to meet the other children coming to Blackhall School in the morning. We called them the village kids and I always remember this girl - I don't know who she was - but she was crying because she was cold, her hands were very cold and I happened to have new gloves on, so I gave them to her, and, of course, I got a good telling off at home because I never said where the gloves had gone.

MISS M. MILLER

The Village in the early 40's

Life wasn't a bed of roses for everybody in Blackhall. No disrespect to any of them in Craigcrook Road - I knew a lot of families there and they knew me, but domestic servants were common place right up until the outbreak of the war. Most of the people living in Keith Crescent had domestic servants - living-in domestic servants. We used to know some of them by their Christian names, there's so-and-so Marshall's domestic and they were as well known as some of the locals. There were a few families in the village that were pretty hard pushed to make ends meet, mainly living in that block almost opposite where the Recreation Hall was with the tunnel - they were living pretty near....... money certainly wasn't very plentiful.

MR. R.BOYCE

That building next to the House O' Hill Pub (Capital Foods Head Office) is still the original, but it had about twice as many houses when we were young. I think they gutted it in the early forties or something and made it into higher class houses, but at one time they were just a room and kitchen with the toilet on the stair. There were houses in the pend too, up at the back and above where MacAndrews is....they were entered from the back stair at both sides and through doors on either side at the entry to the pend, so there was quite a lot of people lived in that bit.

MR. W. WOOD

But expansion from the town continued and in 1920 Blackhall became officially part of Edinburgh.

CHAPTER 6

TRANSPORT

To-day the amount of traffic on the Queensferry and Telford Roads is giving rise to pollution level problems, and even some of the smaller roads are very busy, but, as seen in the previous chapter it was not always that way – 'you got the odd S.M.T. Bus' as can be seen in the pictures below taken around the mid 1930's.

The odd SMT bus coming through Blackhall

Mr. A. MacDonald recalls seeing earlier buses:-

> *I remember seeing, before we came out to Blackhall, the old Queensferry buses going out with their solid tyres and open sides, but by the time we came out to Blackhall they'd got a bit better.*

And there are others who recall transport which went at a much more leisurely pace.

> *I remember the four-in-hand carriages going through the village. As small boys we used to jump on the back step when the horses slowed down for the hill and when we got to the top and heard the driver telling the passengers "Over on the left is Craigcrook Castle" we jumped off or we would have been taken on to Quarry Brae at Davidson's Mains and it was a long walk back.*
>
> *I can't remember the name of the people in Marchfield, Davidson's Mains but they had a coach which occasionally went through the village and the man on the top at the back used to blow the horn.*

> MR. R. RENTON

I was born in 1 Marischal Place on 1st August, 1908. My father had the carter's business, we had horses and carts in where the shops are now, where the Savings Bank is, that used to be Simpson's Dairy – and we had them round where the old school was, before the houses were built that was just fields – the kids had a grand time playing around in them. We had horses in the pend there, we had horses in Simpson's and we had horses at Davidson's Mains and we had horses at Corstorphine. And that last house in Keith Row before you go into the Bowling Green, that was my father's – for his workmen. And that building beside the Roadhouse, above the hairdressers and MacAndrews – that used to be a block of eight houses, it is now four, and my father had two houses there for his workmen, but it has all changed.

Mr. Duncan with one of his horses

He used to run a cab service to the station and that... and he had a wagonette or a brake whatever you liked to call it and he would go to Barnton Station – you couldn't get any further than Barnton Station from the town and he used to drive you from the station down to Cramond foreshore. And there was the general carting, down to Cramond beach to get sand and to the quarries to get sand or gravel and when the roads were being repaired he would bring up the stuff.

MISS B. DUNCAN

When you went your holidays, you got your cab from Duncan's – oh, he was very good and he would come to meet you when you came home, he would say 'when are you coming home? Send me a post card' and he was there waiting for us. We got off at Haymarket, we used to go to Fife and Duncan would be standing there waiting, no bother, no taxis or anything like that. He was very good, he always turned up.

DR. J. HARLAND

Some places haven't changed, like the old pend, where Duncan had his horses and cabs. He used to hire them out and that's one thing that my grandmother enjoyed very much. Just occasionally in the summer time we would hire one of these open cabs and she would thoroughly enjoy a ride round the district in that. And I suppose we must have used them when we were going on holiday to take luggage and things. He must have had ponies and traps for hire too because my father did that twice and took the whole family in an open trap down to East Lothian for holidays and that, as far as I can remember, was hired from Duncan's.

MRS. C. MITTELL

A family outing in an open trap

Alexander Teenan, local baker at the turn of the century, also wrote about the horse-drawn vehicles which passed through the village and gave a lucid view of "Bonnie Blackha" at the same time. Only 12 of his 15 verses are reproduced here.

Frae the West End we start, whar the finger-post stands,
And mixes the traffic wi' its wunderfu' hands;
Cross owre the Dean Brig; whau the Leith waters flow,
That hae tempted a few to the regions below.
Drive further alang on the auld Ferry Road,
Oor Coachman looks happy (complete is his load)
So he doffs his white hat wi' a puff and a blaw,
And describes some of the wonders o' Bonnie Blackha'.

'Twad mak' truith lovin' saunts owre the world wide sneeze;
As that driver's description floats oot on the breeze.
First comes the auld quarry, where in days o' Land Syne,

They howkit the stanes for their buildings sae fine;
Though it's noo only used a bit kittling to droon,
It supplies a' the stanes for the best o' the toon –
The Gladstone Memorial and the grand Usher Ha',
Are o' stanes frae the quarry at Bonnie Blackha'.

Next in turn comes the station, wi' its frontage o' glass,
Where the chimney pots wink owre the sign as ye pass.
It's a beautiful buildin', a magnificent pile,
Gies the N.B. directors a touch o' the bile.
Inside sits the maister, surrounded wi' clerks,
Wi' their silver faced tunics and clean biled serks;
It's bonny to see them a' ranged in a raw
Frae the fit o' the gangway at Bonnie Blackha'.

There's the shop on the left that sells paraffin ile,
Next door to the man wha takes folk tae the jile;
And the wonderful baker, whase troubles are o'er,
Wi' his baps in the morning ye'll see him nae more.
Frae his worries and cares he was suddenly freed,
Wi' financial fever he sickened and de'ed.
Back, back to the city they bore him awa',
But his ghost wanders sometimes to Bonnie Blackha'.

Nae pub can they boast whaur tae get a bit dram,
Which bring forth frae strangers a guid herty "damn";
But across frae the grocer's they've quietly tae mooch,
A red herrin' in their hand, and a gill in their pooch,
And on Sunday when daunderin' oot on the green,
There's nae living mortal on earth tae been seen;
But a hen cannae cackle, nor a cock craw,
But they keek round their curtains at Bonnie Blackha'

There's the shop wi' the pavement in front o' the door,
Aye puts me in mind o' Tim Flannigan's store;
There's flase teeth and treacle, fire shovels and leeks,
And buttons to shoo on yer serks and yer breaks,
Claith, Tatties, and Seybies, Finnan Haddies in Shoals,
A drop o' guid whisky, or a cart o' guid coals,
Baps, bacon, and barley, and 'porter an a',
It drapt like a god send on Bonnie Blackha'.

But we're prood o' oor village there's no the least doot,
Wi' its hydrants and lamp-posts a' scattered aboot;
City folk sometimes say they've a thoot in their croon,
Whaur's Blackha' by and by? – swallowed up by the toon.
But e'en let them swallow – that intelligent feed
Will put sense in their stumack, mair than's noo in their heid,
'Boot their Knichts and their Baronets
                    they brag and they blaw,
But we've a king sellin' codlin's in Bonnie Blackha'.

'The King Sellin' Codlin' now J & S Roberts at the corner of Marischal Place

Noo, a bit faurer on, there's a dairyman croose,
May a blessin' descend on his own thakit hoose!
Fo ye'll find him a man fu' o' guid sterling worth,
And he aye tak's me back to a scene in the north,
The milkmaid sang sweet as her pail she did fill,
And the simmer sun smiled owre the face o' the hill,
While the tap glistened white wi' perpetual snaw,
He's credit to Scotlan' and Bonnie Blackha'.

The kirk o' Columba stands up on the brae,
Whaur they gether for worship each quiet sabbath day;
It's no big as yet, but it's growin betimes,
And some day will possess baith an organ and chimes.
There's a board of instructions placed up at the gate,
But inside o' the door there's nae sign o' a plate,
They've to joggle the pockies the coppers to draw,
For they're juist like their neebours in Bonnie Blackha'

They'd nae burial grund when their relatives died,
But kind co-operation that want has supplied.
When a husband depairts for the braw golden shore
They get coffins and coaches supplied by the "Store";
And the wife tells her weans when they visit his mound,
There lies yer puir faither – fowre and fowre-pence the pund.
We'll hae "Committee Villas" and "Deevidend Raw",
Then we'll reach to perjection at Bonnie Blackha'.

> The driver bein' feenished he gethered his braith,
> And the silence that followed was quieter than daith,
> The Yankee dumfoonder'd looked up to the sky,
> Saw the shade o' George Washington hoverin' nigh,
> Sadly gazed at the coachman and thoct to himself,
> Alone did he do it as he reached the hotel,
> Asked the man at the bar some freshment to draw,
> To synde owre the wonders o' Bonnie Blackha'.

This leisurely form of transport had links with another much noisier, faster and well remembered mode of transport as this extract from an article in the Edinburgh Evening Dispatch of 24th April 1951 makes clear.

> *Another chapter in the history of the British Railways will be closed when the 1.47 pm train leaves Barnton on Saturday, May 5 – the last to leave the station.*
>
> *In its early days the line was quite a busy one, a large number of passengers being golfers. However when the bus route was opened up the popularity of the railway gradually declined.*
>
> *The station was opened on March 1, 1894 and the first train ran on February 28th. Trains were half-hourly. At week-ends there was a quarter-hour service, but now there are only six a day.*
>
> *Before the trains and buses started to run to Barnton, Henry Baillie of Cramond met the trains at Craigleith Station with a gig. Mr. Baillie is now 88 and his son Charles Baillie ran the last coach from Barnton in 1921 after the buses started to run.*

Nearer Blackhall was a 'stop' for those who stayed at the north end of the village.

> *I went to school by train, it was the cheapest way of going – I can't be definite but I think a child could go for a ha'penny up to Princes Street. I had a season ticket. There were quite a lot of us went by train but most started going by bus – it was quite a long walk to the station for the people at the top of the road, but then they opened the House o' Hill Halt, but by that time the bus had really taken over. But it was good going by train, you could sometimes do your lessons, there was more room to move about.*
>
> MISS M. MILLER

> *I used to go to the House o' Hill Halt to get the train to Niddrie when I was teaching there - I took the train to the West End Station and walked up and caught the Niddrie bus at Bread Street. I think the train suited business people, we got into the West End, you see and that suited me from here.*
>
> *And we used to go from Craigleith Station down to friends at Granton.*
>
> MISS J. WRIGHT

> *House o' Hill Halt - the train came from Caledonian, Dalry, Murrayfield, Blackhall and it split after Blackhall and one went to House o' Hill Halt, Davidson Mains and Barnton and the other one went to Pilton and Granton. In my first working period, '37-'39, I worked at the West End in the City Analyst office and we all travelled by train to work, because I was in Stafford Street and, of course, the station was handy and buses were not so common even in the later thirties and nearly all the people who worked in the West End of town travelled by train, it was cheaper than buses too.*
>
> DR. A. ROSS

But it was Craigleith Station which stimulated memories for many Blackhall folk.

Craigleith Station

Anyone looking over the bridge where the Queensferry Road crosses the wooded gully where the railway used to be, might find it difficult to believe that the once busy Craigleith Station occupied the site. The photograph shows how, after passing under the bridge, the line divided, the left hand one (now partly a cycle track) going to Davidson's Mains and Barnton, the right hand one to Granton Road, Newhaven and Leith. Before the buses ran, the trains provided the only public transport to town and even after the buses began to compete, the rail kept its popularity because it was cheaper (1d third class single for a long time, rising to 1½d.)

At peak hours there was standing room only in the city bound carriages which had no corridors, so intending boarders ran up and down the platform looking for a compartment where they could squeeze in. The first stop was at Murrayfield which was reached after crossing a bridge high above the Water of Leith. After Murrayfield Rugby Stadium was built this quiet station used to come to life on International Saturdays, when extra trains conveyed hordes of enthusiasts on their way to the ground. The next station was Dalry Road, when often a good view could be had of engines filling up with coal and water. Finally the terminus was reached at the Caledonian Station at the west end of Princes Street where, during World War 1, passengers were confronted with posters telling them that Kitchener wanted them at the Front.

On the right as you entered Craigleith Station was the booking office where, shortly before the train was due, a shutter was raised and you bought your ticket at a pigeon-hole. The piece of green paste-board was punched in a machine and handed to you; one of the staff at the foot of the stairs checked that you had one and you gave it to a ticket collector at your destination. There were first and third class waiting rooms and a Station Master's Office. Just what happened if a third-class passenger went into the first-class waiting room remains a mystery. The photograph shows a staff of seven. Gradually the numbers were reduced until eventually the station was unmanned; then the trains stopped running and another Blackhall landmark disappeared, although its name lives on as one of the stages in the bus time-tables

MR. D. FRASER
(Blackhall Bulletin 1983)

During the twenties and thirties the majority of secondary school pupils - apart from those attending Daniel Stewart's travelled by train from Craigleith. The train we travelled on came from Barnton and Davidson's Mains and left Craigleith for Princes Street station at 8.28 am...there was always a mad sprint by many of the boys. Murrayfield was just another pick up point, but pupils for Boroughmuir and Tynecastle decanted at Dalry with the former exiting via the Telford Subway and Dundee Street to go up Viewforth and the latter going out to Dalry Road from the other end of the platform. Pupils who carried on to Princes Street Station were those attending Heriots, Queen Street, the old Royal High in Regent Road and James Gillespies Girl's School. A monthly season ticket for pupils cost 3/4d pre-war. We also used the train to go into evening classes, most of us returning home by the 9.57 pm train. Trains were also the main means of transport on Saturdays to Football Matches at Tynecastle and to Rugby Internationals at Murrayfield.

MR. R. BOYCE.

Craigleith Station - we used to come up from Inverleith, when we were down at the Rugby and the Scouts used to go swimming at Dalry Road Baths, so the Davidson's Mains and Barnton people came in on the train and we picked it up at Craigleith, up to Dalry Road and back again.

MR. A. MACDONALD

We went into Queens Street School - Mary Erskine's, my sister and I - by train. It cost you a penny one way and a penny ha'penny for a return, I remember that much. And, of course, we got season tickets. One of the funny things I remember about school was getting out early every day in order to catch the train back to Craigleith because it left at twenty to four....we got it at the Caley Station, there wasn't another train until four fifteen and that was considered a long wait for any child so we actually got out of school five minutes early. And I still remember the times of the trains going in in the morning, there was an eight twenty two that came from Barnton and that was the one we were supposed to get, if we were late we got the eight thirty one which came from Leith and it took eight minutes to Princes Street - to the Caley but you had more of a rush to get down to school on time from that one. That was the one that a lot of people from Granton used to come up to go to Stewart's, my husband used to come up on that train from Trinity and get off at Craigleith and then walked in. Eventually, of course, a lot of us used bicycles to go to school, after the war, you certainly used bicycles because there was so little traffic, it was the easy way, I suppose.

MRS. M. EDINGTON

My sister and I were sent straight into Edinburgh Ladies' College at Atholl Crescent, which has now, of course, become Mary Erskine School. It started off at Atholl Crescent, the elementary school was there and, of course, that was very handy for Caledonian Station. I'll never forget my first day being taken in to the school with my older sister and my father came with us.

MRS C. MITTELL

I went to Boroughmuir on the train - there were only S.M.T. buses and they were every hour - the trains were better. You could get a yearly season for the train - I think it was about fifteen shillings, and then you could go on the train any time you liked.
The first Corporation buses ran to Cramond only, they turned at Cramond and came back, they didn't go to Barnton till after the second war, they started going to Cramond between the wars.

MR. H. ERSKINE

In the 1919 "Rec" Magazine, the following 'Recipe' was given for catching the 8.33 am. train by a gentleman who called himself 'Wunwhoo Hasdunit'.

Take a resolution tall
To get up with the morning lark
Or before it, if you can.
Do not heed base slumbers call,
Even if the morning's dark:
Tumble up and be a man!
Get your shaving done in haste,
Do not cut your beastly chin!
(Be most careful as to this!)
Choose a tie in perfect taste
Therein fix ruby pin!
Ah!...........
Take this counsel in the main,
And you'll catch your morning train,
Every time!

The trains were used so frequently and regularly by people going to work that it seems that friendships were formed between the passengers.

My father went in by train - he was an accountant in an insurance company in Charlotte Square, but he went in and out by train to the office and when he retired in the 1930's, he was given a silver cigarette case by the people who had travelled with him in the train, so that shows the kind of community spirit that existed on the trains.

MISS M. MACDONALD

My husband travelled up and down to Leith in the train - there were quite a few of the men from here worked in Leith and they came home for their lunch and went back again. It was a nice community.

ANON

The trains were a great thing, when I got married, my wife trundled the pram down the station steps and we would put it in the guards van and ride into the Caley or Dalry, or Leith or Granton.....it was well used. They made a great mistake in not retaining those railway lines.

MR. W. WOOD

What I do remember about the trains is the exhibitions that used to come, they would be held in the train, we used to go and look at them instead of coming straight home from school. The Royal train used to come occasionally and you could go on it. You could hire a coach rather like a caravan and use it as a camping holiday but, of course, it was on the railways.

I remember the station had these machines that if you put your penny in, it would pick up things and drop it through the opening for you - we enjoyed finding out what we had got.

MISS M. MILLER.

We moved into Blackhall in November 1969 but I'd lived in Craigleith Hill for 6 years before that. I remember walking from school and seeing Craigleith Station being taken apart. You went into the booking office from the Queensferry Road and then down from there - not that I ever really used the train.....but it was strange to see the Station go.

MRS. E. STUART

The platform is still visible at the side of the Cycle Track

BLACKHALL NOSTALGIA

We used to have a railway train
That whizzed across the city
With flags and guards and happy seats;
But now, alas, the pity,
The station's gone, the friends are split
That chatted about wickets,
And moths and butterflies make do
with weeds and bramble thickets.

We used to have a farmstead here
with calves and lowing cattle;
But now we have a frightsome road

And cars that screech and rattle.
There isn't even a proper span
to let us cross at leisure.
'Please take my hand, the pip-pip's gone
Seven seconds is their pleasure.'

Still, lift your eyes and cross with care,
Suppressing all those cusses.
And what reward if you last out?
Free passes on the buses.

MRS. M. HALLIDAY.

CHAPTER 7

THE BUILDING OF THE CHURCHES

Blackhall is now fortunate enough to have two churches in its midst - St. Columba's and the United Free Church - and their presence is due to the hard work and continued perseverance of many people. As **St. Columba's** is the older of the two churches, we will look at its history first.

St. Columba's Church

As already mentioned in a previous chapter, Blackhall was trisected by the Parish boundaries of three churches - Cramond, Corstorphine and St. Cuthbert's - but the religious services in the village were actually performed by other churches, as Mr. A.S. Denholm, writing in the Rec Magazine of 1918 makes clear.

> *Many years ago when Blackhall was a little village of a few houses and the population naturally much less than it is now, the inhabitants were wont to gather for religious service on Sunday evenings to a small meeting house in what was then known as "Paddy's Row." This was a small house, with the partition dividing the "but and ben" removed and provided with forms to seat about fifty people.*
>
> *The meeting house was the property of the Gartshores of Ravelston and all expenses for lighting, heating, etc were born by them. We hear much to-day about the union of the churches, but even in the far off days of which we write, we find three churches working together in pefect harmony. Free St. Stephen's Church had the biggest share in the religious activities of the village. They carried on a Mission Sunday School and a Penny Savings bank and also along with Dean Parish Church and Dean Free Church provided speakers for the Sunday evening services.*

In 1885 the meeting house was re-converted into a dwelling house, the Sunday School, Bank and religious service finding a new home in the handsome hall erected by Miss Murray Gartshore in memory of her father.

Miss Gartshore not only built the hall but also provided a missionary who conducted the services and visited the people in their homes. On the departure of Mr. Malcolm (the missionary) the three churches already mentioned, once more carried on the services, being now assisted by Cramond Free Church, which also for several years carried on a Band of Hope here.

We had a fine organ in the hall which was ably played by Miss Ferrier. We were indebted in those days to Mr. Urquhart, precentor of Free St. Stephen's and Mr. Denholm, precentor, Dean Free, for bringing out their choirs occasionally and giving us a musical treat, also to St. Stephen's for their Sunday School soiree, which everybody, even the oldest inhabitant, attended. It may seem strange that Cramond Parish Church had no part in these matters, but at that time Blackhall was divided into three parishes namely, St. Cuthbert's, Corstorphine and Cramond and the only two houses in Cramond Parish were Mr. J.C. Simpson's and Mr. A.S. Denholm's.

Cramond Parish Church had, however, a great deal to do with the establishing of a church in Blackhall, as the following extracts from Cramond Session Minutes of 1898/99 show:-

OCTOBER 1898 -The Moderator brought before the Kirk Session the necessity of Church extension at Blackhall in consequence of the rapid feuing in that district. The Session were unanimously of the opinion that steps should be taken to provide religious ordinances for the new population, and it was resolved to approach the Kirk Session of Dean and Corstorphine on the matter.

JANUARY 1899 - The Moderator read to the Session the correspondence betwixt the Kirk Sessions of Cramond, Corstorphine and Dean regarding the proposed Church extension at Blackhall, and the Kirk Session instructed the Moderator to lay the whole matter before the Presbytery for advice.

This appeal to Presbytery was necessary as Dean Parish Church, which had been built in 1870, and in whose parish most of Blackhall then lay, had raised objections to the building of a Church at Craigcrook. Firstly, because the Kirk Session there felt that as their church was only 1½ miles from Blackhall, there was no need for another church and that many of their regular attenders came from Blackhall. Secondly, Miss Murray Gartshore paid a quarter of their assistant's salary, because he was taking part in the pastoral care of Blackhall, and there was concern that she would withdraw this support, if Blackhall had its own church. And thirdly, the Dean Church were in the process of erecting a 'new handsome church which will meet the increasing necessities of the parish.... at a cost of £800'. It was thought by their Kirk Session that if another church were erected at Blackhall, they would lose a considerable number of their members and the success of their enterprise would be endangered. However, the Prebystery of Edinburgh did not see it that way, as Cramond Session Minutes indicate.

NOVEMBER 1899 - The Moderator reported that the Presbytery had unanimously approved of what had been done and authorised the Session to go on with the erection of the church at Blackhall. The Moderator further reported that he had received plans and specifications for an iron church to be erected at Blackhall from Messrs Speirs & Co, Glasgow, at an inclusive cost of £387 10/-. and also that he had approached the Craigcrook Trustees with a view to getting a site on their estate at a cheaper rate than the ordinary feu duty, and that the Trustess had agreed to give a site for a church at £15 per acre, being half the usual feu duty. He further reported that he had received the promise of subscriptions from a few members of the congregation amounting to £130.10/-., and that a grant of £62.10/-. might be confidently expected from the Home Mission Committee. The Moderator also reported that he had been in communication with the Rev. W.B. Stevenson M.A., Minister of Athelstaneford, with the view of inducing him to accept an appointment as first minister of the new charge at Craigcrook, and he read letters which he had received regarding Mr. Stevenson.

The Session unanimously and cordially approved of the Moderator's proceedings and resolved to request the Rev. Stevenson to undertake the pastorate of the church, the Kirk Session binding themselves to secure a site of not less than half an acre, for which they will pay one year's feu duty, and to erect thereon an iron church costing not more than £400 and to make application to the Home Mission Committee for an annual grant towards the Minister's Stipend. The Kirk Session in making this offer cannot undertake to guarantee any further outlay than that specified above, but should Mr. Stevenson accept their offer, it is their desire and intention that he should have the fullest liberty with regard to the choice of site and erection of church, and the entire conduct of the same.

The Laying of the foundation stone of the permanent church,
the iron church can be seen on the right of the picture

JANUARY 1900 - The Moderator reported as to the Rev. Mr. Stevenson's resignation of his ministry at Athelstaneford preparatory to his taking up the duties of Minister of the new church at Craigcrook.

St. Columba's was consecrated on 4th March, 1900 with Mr. MacLean, the minister of Cramond, conducting the morning service and Mr. Stevenson, the evening service. The church being crowded on both occasions.

Initially the new church must have struggled financially for in January, 1901 a special service and collection was held to help to pay Mr. Stevenson's stipend. However, the congregation quickly enlarged and by 1902 nearly all the sitting accommodation was taken up and it was resolved at a congregational meeting held in March of that year to obtain plans and raise the necessary funds for a permanent church. Mr. MacGregor Chalmers was the appointed architect. He prepared plans for a church to seat 500 with the possibility of being extended to accommodate 900 if the district continued to expand.

The first sod was cut by Mrs. Croall of Craigcrook Castle on the 4th April 1903 and the Foundation Stone laid by His Grace the Lord High Commissioner, Lord Leven & Melville, on 23rd May. The customs relating to the laying of foundations stones were carried out. A casket, containing coins, newspapers of the day along with the Congregational Supplement giving an account of the movement which led to the building of the church, was presented by Mr. Sturrock, the church treasurer, and deposited by His Grace in the cavity. The mortar bed having been laid previously by the workmen.

The Architect's drawing of St. Columba's

A trowel was then presented by the architect, Mr. MacGregor Chalmers. His Grace spread the mortar and the stone was lowered into position. The builder, Mr. Turner, presented a mallet, which was used by His Grace who tapped the stone three times. Mr. Chalmers then presented a square and level and explained its use. His Grace applied it to the stone and declared it well and truly laid.

The ancient ceremony of pouring corn, wine and oil on the stone was then carried out, corn being poured by Lady Leven and Melville, the wine by Mrs. Gillespie and the oil by Mrs. Stevenson.

In the October Church Supplement of that year, Mr. Stevenson wrote the following:-

The Building Fund

For the information of those who have recently come to the district, it may be stated that the cost of the Church including architect's fees etc., is expected to be not less than £4,500. Towards this sum nearly £1,500 has been raised by the Congregation and friends. The usual Home Mission and Baird Trust grants are expected to amount to £1,200, leaving a sum of £1,800 still to be raised. Contributions will be gladly received by the treasurer.

The New Church, consisiting of the nave, north aisle and vestry, was dedicated and opened for worship on Saturday, 28th May, 1904. Dr. Macgregor offered the dedicatory prayer and Principal Story preached the sermon. There was a large and representative congregation numbering over 300 and the collection which was in aid of the building fund amounted to £14.

Several Gifts had been presented to the new church:-

Six stain glass windows in the east end of the church, in memory of the late Robert Croall Esq., of Craigcrook Castle, by his widow and family.
Oak pulpit, in memory of the late Rev. R.H. Stevenson, D.D., minister of St. George's, Edinburgh, by his widow and family.
Communion Table by the Dowager Lady Liston Foulis.
Font in memory of her parents by Mrs. W.B. Stevenson.
Pulpit frontal and Book Markers by Mrs. W.B. Stevenson.
Set of four offertory bags by Mrs. Croall.
Brass plate to receive the offertory by C. Strang Watson, Esq.
Communion Plate by the Misses Denniston Brown, Balloch Castle, in memory of their parents.
Communion Linen by Mrs. Croall.

The Congregational report given in July of the same year showed a very active church.

The congregation which was formed in March 1900 numbered about 150. During the four years that the congregation had existed, 53 have been admitted into the church by baptism, and 37 have been received as first communicants. The number of communicants on the roll at 31st December, 1903 was 186. A Kirk Session has been formed in connection with that of Cramond, consisting of the minister and 6 elders.

A Bible Class and Sunday School have been conducted since the commencement, the number on the roll of the latter being now 111, with a staff of 11 teachers. A Boys Brigade was conducted for the first three years with an excellent attendance and will be resumed next September in the Church Hall. The meetings could not be held this year owing to the want of a suitable hall. The Young Men's Guild which was formed last summer, has had a very successful session and has now 22 on the roll. The praise has been led by an excellent choir now numbering 18, under Mr. T. Morrison, organist, and a singing class for the younger children has been conducted since the commencement by Miss Muir. Work parties have been carried on each year and for the last two years Joinery Classes, and a Savings Bank (formerly managed by St. Stephen's U.F.Y.W.C.A), have been added to the work of the congregation.

During the last year the members and friends have been actively engaged in preparing for the Bazaar that is to be held in December in aid of the Building Fund of the New Church.

The above Bazaar was held over three days and raised the magnificent sum of £1,735.6.1. almost clearing the debt accrued by the building of the church. However it was not until October, 1907 that the debt was finally cleared.

The Rev. W.B.Stevenson continued to lead St. Columba's until November, 1912 when he accepted a five year appointment to be Organising Secretary of the Foreign Mission Committee (work he had been initially seconded temporarily to do from St. Columba's the previous year). He spoke of the long and prayerful consideration the matter had received before he made up his mind to make the wrench from his work in connection with St. Columba's.

Naturally there are few, if any, still living in Blackhall who can remember the days of his ministry, but when he died in 1928, the following tribute was paid to him by Mr. Snadden, minister of St. Columba's at that time.

"He made a great sacrifice coming to Blackhall twenty eight years ago. He left a quiet, peaceful, beautiful parish to build up a congregation here, where there was no congregation and no church. It was hard, uphill, worrying work which few ministers would have faced. But face it he did with courage and confidence and soon there were gathered around him a devoted congregation, and with characterisitic energy and perseverance he built the fine church in which we worship to-day. It will always stand as his memorial, and his alone, so that in years to come, whoever lives to see it in its completed form, his name will be remembered with it.

The congregation ensured that his name would be remembered by erecting a bronze plaque in the vestibule of the church, which proclaimed him 'a true friend and devoted pastor'.

He was succeeded by the Rev. Cecil T. Thornton who was inducted and ordained to St. Columba's on 12th February, 1913. Mr. Thornton's stay in Blackhall was comparatively short due to the 1914-18 War as he 'gave up his ministry on 16th May 1916 to go and serve his country.'

The next occupant, the Rev. D. Wilson Baird came from a background in the Presbyterian Church of England. His ministry was also comparatively short as he resigned on September 14th, 1920 to go to Augustine Parish Church, Greenock. The Church Membership at that time stood at 291.

> *We used to go to the church at Davidson's Mains when we first came. St. Columba's wasn't a parish church then, and it was a Mr. Baird who was the minister and he asked my father if he would come to Blackhall Church and help out, so we changed to Blackhall*
>
> MRS. H. STURGEON

The Rev. Andrew M. Snaddon was called to St. Columba's from Gilmerton Church. He was inducted on 8th May, 1921 and seems to have had a rather dynamic personality, for five months after his arrival, 24 young communicants joined the church and a further sixty joined by certificates of transference. In that same month, October, he also inaugurated plans to raise St. Columba's to a Parish Church status instead of being an adjunct to Cramond Parish Church. To become a Parish Church, it was necessary that the congregation should raise the sum of 30,000 shillings and Mr. Snaddon started 'the ball rolling' by giving the first 1,000 shillings himself. Once more the church set to work with a will and by June 1922, the sum of £1,649:10:10. had been raised, and on 31st July, 1922, St. Columba's Church was 'erected into a Parish.'

Other changes also took place. In 1928 electric lighting was installed in the Church by Mr. E. Rolland MacNab in memory of his wife. The Badminton Club of 1930 was responsible for providing electric lighting in the Church Hall.

Mr. Snadden went into semi-retirement in 1931, and the Rev. Frederick Sim was appointed his assistant and successor. At that time the church membership stood at 656 and the need to raise money for an extension to the church was being felt. In 1932, a pipe organ was installed and the choir gallery erected at a cost of £1,250, but this was still found to be insufficient and once more the congregation set to work to raise funds.

> *Before the South transcept was built, you could tell that the church had been cut short in its building, because it was a rough temporary wall with the odd stone. There used to be a scale model of the church, an architect's model, and it stood on a table just near the door through to where the church office is now. It showed the church as it was intended, complete with its steeple coming up and it looked really lovely. Every time I went into church when I was in the B.B.s and Sunday School I used to stand and admire this model, it fascinated me - I've often wondered what happened to it.*
>
> MR. R. BOYCE

> *There was a lot of extension work - the gallery and that, and then the halls. When I was married in 1934 the tarpaulin was up where they were putting in the gallery. It's really grown - at one time the Communion just filled half the church a way down at the front.*
>
> MRS. H. STURGEON

The building of the South Transcept

I can remember the extension, I've a memory of big sheets of canvas hanging in the church while the extension was being done behind it, but then you see that was what about '35 or '36 or something like that.

MRS. M. EDINGTON

On May 2nd, 1935, the new extension, consisting of the South Aisle (with gallery overhead) and the Session Room (now the church office) with choir room above, was dedicated. This venture had cost £4,500 almost as much as the original church.

Mr. Snadden died at Bishopbriggs in 1936, age 73 years and Mr. Sim became Senior Minister.

I've a vague recollection of Mr. Snaddon who was there before Mr. Sim. I don't remember this but I believe when he was collecting money for the extension, he himself went round every house in the Parish.

MISS M. MACDONALD

Mr. Snadden was here when we first came, then Mr. Sim came as his colleague and successor I think was the term used. Well, I suppose Mr. Snadden went into semi retirement and then he retired completely after a few years.

MR. A. MACDONALD

Rev. F.R. Sim (assistant 1931-36, senior minister 1936-45) showed a keen interest in the children's and youth organisations and he will be remembered as a very popular guest at the Christmas parties where he was particularly noted for organising a game known as 'O'Grady!' During Mr. Sim's ministry in 1933 a new manse was purchased at 5 Blinkbonny Crescent and this has now been in use for 46 years.

DR. J. HARLAND
(Blackhall Bulletin 1984)

One of my memories of Mr. Sim was that he and Mrs. Sim came to the house and he gave me a penny for keeping quiet for five minutes.

MRS. M. EDINGTON

Mr. Sim continued to minister to the congregation until his death on August 4th, 1945 and the following tribute appear in the Congregational News.

In 1931, he came to Blackhall, mature in experience of life, with a knowledge of men and affairs beyond that of many ministers. His unmistakable abilities and gospel fervour were blessed by God to the speedy building up and strengthening of all the congregational activities. He took over a membership roll of 600: to-day the number is fully doubled. The necessary additions to the Church fabric happily completed without detriment to its noble lines were made possible by the minister's directing energy and initiative. The Church organisations were multiplied and all infused by his bouyant and enthusiastic spirit.......We look back then with thanksgiving and praise to God on a life well fulfilled in the highest services man can render to his master and to his fellow men. His passing lay a deep sense of loss on this Church and the whole parish community.

In 1946, he was succeeded by the Rev. James G. Matheson, who came as the son of a Free Chuch of Scotland manse and an Army Chaplain, with a successful reputation in youth work. His ministry in Blackhall was a comparatively short one, but according to the June issue of the Congregational News of 1951, 'one of the most outstanding in the history of the parish'. The tribute continued:-

True it is that the success of Mr. Matheson's ministry here might superficially be measured in ordinary standards by the growth in the size of the congregation (from 1150 to 1396) by the admissions of new communicants (130), by the number and dimensions of the various ancillary groups (Youth Fellowship, Sunday School, Woman's Guild and Men's Group), several of which owe their initiation to his leadership, tact and organising ability. But in our view the real measure of his success is to be found in the enthusiastic response of the people of his parish to his gospel teaching, and to the practical Christianity which he explains and expounds to an ever expanding congregation, a congregation continually activated by his sincerity of purpose, his modesty of approach and his appreciation of the world in which we live.

Members still living in the area have also good memories of his ministry.

It wasn't until that last big re-union of the Youth Fellowship, when his wife Nicky said to me "Oh what you did for him when he came here was absolutely tremendous" I had never thought of it that way round, I had always thought of what he did for us, because as youngsters we were so indebted to him in so many ways. I remember he came with us the first time we went to Iona. A whole group of us went, which was maybe wrong because it was too big a group, we were overpowering in the set-up. It wasn't until the

Thursday when he got shaved and put on his dog-collar, because that was the night of the dance, that the other folk knew that he was actually the minister. I feel I was more influenced by him than anybody.

MRS. M. EDINGTON

Jim Matheson made a tremendous impact and unfortunately I was just a year or two too old to have got into the Youth Fellowship, because I think I would have enjoyed that very much. He had a very, very good clear voice, probably still has, and I remember we did several broadcast services....I think probably because he was such a good preacher and he had this clear voice.

MISS M. MACDONALD

As far back as 1939, the kirk session had decided that the church hall was no longer adequate and a hall fund, which could be contributed to by regular monthly givings was set up. However this fund was very slow to grow, probably due to the exigencies of war and its aftermath, but the old 'tin kirk' was well used and holds many memories for some of Blackhall's inhabitants.

Then there was the B.B.'s in the old tin hall - not the posh building that's there nowadays - and at one time they had a rifle range in it. All sorts of things went on in the hall - that's where we had most of our entertainment. Of course, it was a much smaller community then. The old church hall was right at the back, it was hidden practically by the church, you could see the bottom end of it. We used to enter it from behind the church

MR. W. WOOD

One of the plays performed in the old hall

The old church hall was back from the road - it was a great wee hall and there was a lot done in that hall. The Whist Drives that we used to have, you've no idea. There used to be a sewing class and we all had to make something and sew tea-cloths - I remember we made £99 one time with the sale of our work. When the Kirk Social was on, Mr. Simpson from the dairy used to get up on his feet and talk about how there should have been a spire on the kirk and they used to tell him to sit down for they'd heard it a thousand times before....the fun we used to have at those Social.

MRS. H. STURGEON

After the war they bought an old army hut and put it up as additional hall accommodation - really for the Sunday School, then all that was cleared away. The Sunday School seemed quite big in our day, certainly bigger than it is now. Our children were in that hut when they were in Sunday School.

MR. A. MACDONALD

The old tin Kirk had a bell on it....and Sandy Kerr who stayed in Keith Row, he used to be the church officer and he used to ring the church bell. Of course there's no bell to ring now and there hasn't been since that hall disappeared because the tower was never completed.

MR. R. BOYCE

In the March issue of the 1946 Church Supplement, the following obituary appeared for the above Church Officer

During the past month Mr. A.C. Kerr passed to his rest. For 52 years he was resident in Blackhall, and was Church Officer of St. Columba's for the long period of forty two years, retiring from duty several years ago. When he first came to Blackhall, there was no church, and a Service was normally held in the Blackhall Recreation Rooms. Mr. Kerr rendered valuable and faithful service during his long connection with our church, and we extend our sincere sympathy to Mrs. Kerr and family in their sorrow.

It was during the ministry of the Rev. R.J. Watson Mathewson, who came in 1952, that the hall fund received a new impetus. At the Annual General Meeting in February, 1953 a three year plan was launched with the view of raising a Capital Fund of £20,000, to cover the cost of a new hall, a new heating installation and new communion glasses. It was hoped that each member would give 5/-. a week towards the fund. Whether or not each member did so is not stated, but by June 1955, a model of the new hall was available for the congregation to view, and on 31st March, 1957, the hall was officially opened and dedicated by the then Moderator of the General Assembly, The Right Rev. Dr. R.F.V. Scott. The cost of the building was £25,000 of which £20,000 had already been raised by direct giving from the congregation.

Mr. Mathewson came to Blackhall from Cathcart Street Church, Ayr and served St. Columba's for 24 years, sadly having to resign due to continual ill health. At his farewell service in 1975, the then Moderator, the Very Rev. James Matheson spoke of him as a very special minister who would be difficult to replace and tribute was paid to his courage and contagious faith.

Mr. Mathewson was succeeded by the Rev. Ernest G. Sangster, who came from

Beechgrove Church, Aberdeen in June, 1976. Under his ministry, the hall accommodation had to be once more extended, St. Columba's Halls being very much a Community Centre for Blackhall. This extension cost £45,000 and was formally opened by the Very Rev. Dr. James Matheson on the 19th November, 1978. Mr. Sangster ministered to St. Columba's for 14 years and left to go to Alva Parish Church in 1990, and tribute was paid to the care he had taken of the congregation, particularly in joyous and sad occasions and to the amount of care he took in preparing each service.

In March, 1991, Rev. Alex Douglas came from Kingcase Church, Prestwick to become the new minister of St. Columba's.

BLACKHALL UNITED FREE CHURCH

Blackhall United Free Church

It was the evangelical fervour of the Rev Alfred Merriweather of Matryrs & St. John's, which led to the establishing of an United Free Church of Scotland in Blackhall. It was during 1933 that the site was purchased. In the monthly record of Martyr' & St. John's, (December, 1933), Mr. Merriweather presented an invitation and a challenge to his members. The motto which was chosen for the year was "Have Faith in God". It was initmated that an empty shop opposite the site had been rented for the whole of 1934. It was in this shop (12 Telford Road) that the first services of Blackhall United Free Church of Scotland were held on 14th January, 1934. During the week that followed there was a service each evening and friends brought gifts to complete the furnishings such as a piano and hymn books.

On 23rd January, 1934, there was a meeting of ladies called to form a Women's Meeting known as the Blackhall Women's Fellowship. This organisation is still meeting and well attended on alternate Tuesdays.

The Memorial Stone of the building was unveiled on 12th October, 1935 by Mrs. Forrestor-Paton (Alloa) and the new hall was opened on 29th February, 1936 by Mrs. William Dunn (Newport).

The Rev. R.S.C. Blance in Australia, their first student pastor, wrote the following article in a 1975 booklet celebrating their fortieth anniversay:-

I was fortunate to be appointed to Blackhall in 1934 because Blackhall village was a developing area and a well disposed and interested congregation (Matyrs' and St. John's, Edinburgh) backed me up in my work.

I was promised all the help I needed in furthering the cause of the U.F. Church in Blackhall and district, and the church not only kept their word but exceeded their promise.

The cause had been widely and solidly established by the minister of Matyrs' and St. John's, the Rev. Alfred Merriweather who keenly participated in the work and was strongly supported by a genial Martyrs' elder, Mr. Robert Robertson, a retired business man who live in Morningside, who gave unstinting help and supplied whatever was needed to forward the cause.

The members worked in a shop in Telford Road and were an enthusiastic and dedicated group.

The Sunday School numbered 13 and we thought that this would be a good point from which to make a forward thrust, since houses were being built all round us and young families were settling in.

During the summer I made a door to door visitation through the area from Groathill to Davidson's Mains. When the Sunday School took up, the children responded and we were pretty crowded. We certainly did need a Hall, and 120 children went over to the hall when the great day came. The children were as keen as any for the new building, and collected in their bags, then on the day the Foundation Stone was laid, they handed over their gifts and laid their bricks in place.

We had first class helpers in our Blackhall Group, but we did appreciate the help our Martyrs' Church gave - Miss Wright, an experienced teacher taking charge of the Kindergarten; Alfred (now Dr. Merriweather) leading a week day group of children in Bible Study; while Mr. Armstrong, a young elder from Martyrs' thrilled the children with his lantern talks on Saturday evenings. A Scout Group was formed and met under the stage in the hall. Miss Alison Thomson staged Biblical Dramas with children as actors; the choir was gathered - a great help to worship on Sunday.

In the Village Hall, a Men's Meeting was set up. The men met once a month and many interesting speakers came, including the Earl of Home.

The ladies, led by Mrs. B.G. MacGregor, with Mrs. Muir, Miss Bayne, Mrs. Scott, Mrs. Paterson and Mrs. A.B. Robertson, to mention only a few, were constantly active in extending the work, and raising funds for the Hall; Garden Parties helped the finances and also a closer fellowship and deeper sense of belonging.

The church made a deep impact on the community for they were a prayerful group, and the midweek Prayer Meeting was always an event.

For me, Blackhall was an enlarging experience and I shall always remember to be grateful for those who so greatly deepened the enrichment of my spiritual life.

Others in the booklet also recall those early days:-

I always say that I began my missionary service in an empty shop, used as a temporary church in Blackhall. And it was quite a lowly beginning! I was the lantern operator at the Saturday evening young people's meeting. It was in the days of the old magic lantern which thrilled the youngsters in the days when there was no television to distract them. Miss Leila Wright was the pianist and the youngsters used to love to sing the old choruses such as 'Wide, wide as the ocean'. Occasionally a misionary speaker would come and thrill us with tales of Africa or India.

It was a great day for the young Blackhall Church when the Hall was opened. It was packed with people from all U.F. Churches in Edinburgh, and I can still remember the feeling of excitement and enthusiasm which was present and I can still hear in my imagination the applause which greeted my father's announcement, after the offertory had been counted, that the Hall was now free of Debt!

DR. A.M. MERRIWEATHER.

Those of us who were privileged to be associated with the early days of the Blackhall congregation will no doubt agree that their vague, if well meaning ideas of the Church's mission would never have reached fruition without the leadership and evangelical fervour of Rev. Alfred Merriweather.....

As I recall there were afternoon and evening services held in the shop and these were conducted by Elders, retired Ministers and on occasions by Ministers in the Presbytery........

In the meantime plans were being made for the erection of a Church Hall and a Building Fund was started. The condition of the feu required it be built within ten years but the coming of the Second World War and its aftermath not only delayed the implementation of the plans but completely altered them. On reflection one feels this may not have been all adverse. Building costs of the 30's are not comparable to those of today but the whole undertaking called for sacrificial giving and enthusiastic fund raising on the part of the Martyrs' and St. John's Congregation. It must be placed on record that there was no diminution of the giving to the Congregational needs or the wider work of the church.

MR. JAMES MATHER

An extension to the building was added and opened on 31st May, 1969 due to exceptional effort on the part of the office bearers and congregation. This made it possible for the congregation to have a permanently furnished Church.

The ministers who have served the church over these years are - Rev. R.S.C. Blance, Rev. G.B. Smith, Rev. D.W. Roy, Rev. J.G. Grant, Rev. C. M. Greig and the Rev. Ronald Thomson is the present minister.

SCHOOLDAYS

At one point in Blackhall's history there were three schools in the village.

There were two what you might call private preparatory schools in Blackhall - one was Miss Berry's who was above what is now the hairdresser or Chinese Restaurant just down from the butcher's - in the middle of that block. And there was another one which was almost at the bus stop on the other side of what is now Seaforth Terrace and there was a great deal of rivalry between the two as to which one was the best. I was only in the Miss Berry one and my recollection was that there were about ten or twelve in the school but I don't know about the other one. It was just the three 'Rs' we were taught and I had no trouble getting into Stewart's following that, I jumped the first two classes in Stewart's. In those days you either walked to Stewart's or you had a bicycle but nowadays I see they all get their pennies for the bus.

DR. A. ROSS

I started my schooling when I was 5 at a private school, Miss Mathers, which was in 1 Seaforth Terrace and it was two sisters who ran it. They also taught piano because I remember in the second year getting piano lessons there. It was a preparatory school for two years and I remember I was quite a good reader and good at arithmetic and things like that. I've no recollection of having any handicrafts or painting or anything, but I think I was quite happy there and then I went on to what was then Edinburgh Ladies' College in Queen's Street.

MISS M. MACDONALD

I went to Miss Mather's little school when I was five and stayed until I was seven. We met first of all in her house and then we moved to the church hall, because the school got too big for her house. I can remember that at a certain time all work stopped and you got a very small portion of a Bourbon biscuit and then you went back to your work. It was a very good preparatory school, when I went along to Daniel Stewart's I was put far too high up and my father went along a while later and said that he wanted me back a class, it was too far up - so that shows how well she had prepared me. I think there was maybe about fifteen or so in the school, and it didn't matter what school they went to - they always got a very, very glowing tribute to whoever had educated them before.

DR. J. HARLAND

And Blackhall Primary School was sometimes used as a preparatory school as well.

I went to Blackhall School for a couple of years and then I went on to Daniel Stewart's. Miss Lumsden was the headmistress when I was there. I started in 1942, and Miss Wright was my teacher.

MR. D.J. MCLEAN

I went to Blackhall School - everybody started at Blackhall School. There was Miss Aitken, Miss Geddes and Miss Swan. Most of them went as far as the Qualifying and then went to another school, but I went to Stewarts when I was seven.

MR. W. WOOD

E H Ranson & Co now occupy the Murray Gartshore Hall
which was the first official school building

Blackhall School Logbook commences on the 3rd of October, 1902. It does not state where the school building was situated, simply that the schoolroom measured 38ft by 21ft 6ins., there were 37 pupils and the teacher was called Lilias T. Urquhart.

In October 1904, the Inspector's report read as follows:-

The school is conducted in a pleasant and well appointed building by a very competent teacher and the children are very thoroughly taught. The classes are distinctly proficient in elementary branches and the method by which routine infant instruction can be brightened are understood and practised.

Local residents recall that the school was originally held in the Murray Gartshore Hall.

The original school was in Marischal Place - it was only a primary school and when the pupils got to a certain age they went to Roseburn School until the new school was built in Queen's Road.

MR. R. RENTON

The school was in the Murray Gartshore Hall to begin with - only the small children went there. I was one of the first to go to the new school building in Queen's Road, but it's been demolished now.

MISS G. DODDS

The Inspector's Report of 1906 comments that 'several of the pupils are too old for their stage of attainment (which may have given rise to pupils being sent to Roseburn School) but that reading, writing and arithmetic are excellent. The religious knowledge of the children of that period certainly appears to be much greater than those of to-day, judging by the report of the Rev. W.B. Stevenson, minister of St. Columba's, in 1907.

I examined the children to-day in religious knowledge, including the narrations of the Creation, the Deluge, the life of Joseph, the life of Christ (including some of the miracles) Questions 1-13 of the Shorter Catechism, The Ten Commandments and six hymns and psalms. The answers were remarkably good and the children showed not only an excellent knowledge of the work done, but very considerable brightness and intelligence. I consider that Religious Instruction is very well given in the school.

In that same year, doubts were being expressed about the suitability of the Memorial Hall as school premises and plans made for the building of a new school for the district. There is no record of an official opening but in the School Log of 15th September, 1908 there is this 'master of understatement'

The boarded up school prior to demolition

School has been going on for three weeks. The work of the school has not quite settled down yet, attendance is excellent. The workmen have not yet left the building and the noise is a little distracting.

On 11th January, 1914, Miss Jane Aitken of Davidson's Mains School was appointed to take the Supplementary Class. She became headmistress in January, 1917 and continued in that post until she retired on 22nd April 1940. She was held in very high esteem by her former pupils.

The class of 1919 – Miss Aitken can be seen on the right

I remember Miss Aitken was the headmistress and she lived in that house Roseberry across the road from the church - she used to have a brightly coloured floral basket hanging above the door.

Miss Aitken was a very good teacher, very understanding and a deeply religious woman too, because she played quite a prominent part in the life of the Blackhall Church in her time. But she used to tell us about the wartime, you know, about how the Forbes brothers, Ecky and Bobby, went off to the First World War and how she felt when her ex pupils went off to the Army.

MR. R. BOYCE

Miss Aitken really was a super teacher, she sort of instilled knowledge into you despite yourself almost, she really was great and was a terrible miss when she left.

MISS E. DENHOLM

Miss Aitken was a lovely woman....very sensible, full of common sense, she taught you all sorts of things....she was an example to everybody.

MR. W. WOOD

Miss Aitken was the greatest teacher I ever met in my life. She knew more about teaching than any of them at Boroughmuir - though Boroughmuir was a good school, they taught you well and in those days you had Lowers and Highers.

We had a school football team and we played in the field there that was also a grazing field for Duncan's horses in the summer time. Miss Aitken was our trainer.

She was a great woman, during the War, I was home on leave in 1940, I'd just lost a destroyer in the Irish Sea and was on survivor's leave, so I came to Blackhall and thought I'd go and see Miss Aitken, so I up to Roseberry and knocked on the door and very pleased to see me. Funnily enough I wasn't long back at sea when I heard that she was very ill.

MR. H. ERSKINE

CHURCH SUPPLEMENT APRIL 1957

In the death of Miss Jane Aitken St. Columba's loses a much loved member, and the community one who, over a long period of years played a leading part particularly in work among the young. Miss Aitken was the headmistress at Blackhall Primary School from 1917 to 1940 and a Sunday School teacher and Bible Class leader in our congregation. There must be hundreds of her former pupils in many parts of the world who remember with affection and gratitude as we do, this happy natured devoted soul who has entered into her rest. Our sympathy is extended to her two sisters in their loss
REV R. J. WATSON MATHEWSON.

Under her leadership the school progressed happily and continued to grow. In the late thirties, Maidencraig Crescent was built, giving access to the school directly from the village rather than going along Seaforth Drive and down Queen's Road. Even in the forties it was still a rural school with different age groups in the one class, but the ever increasing population was beginning to cause problems.

A Class in 1948

I started teaching in Blackhall in 1943 and was there until 1948 and there must have been about 140 children there then. The children had to eat their school dinners in the cloakroom - they used to put up tables and the children all crammed in there.

The building of the huts at the school made a difference - it helped a lot, the second year children were put out to the huts and sometimes the babies were in that first hut, but, of course, I wasn't there for very long

MISS J. WRIGHT

The expanding community and the lack of a school/dining hall continued to be a problem for a great number of years. The Report of the Inspector of Education in 1952/53 stated:-

The Roll continues to rise steadily: at date of inspection it had reached 190.

The lower corridor is used as a dining hall. The upper corridor is used each morning as a classroom. The approach to the entrance facing Maidencraig Crescent, used by the majority of pupils is dangerous and requires attention. There are no appliances for dealing with an outbreak of fire. There are no road warning signs in the vicinity of the school.

Despite all these defects, the Inspector also noted that 'The general atmosphere and work of the school were pleasing and reflected credit on the recently retired headmistress and on the present headmistress and her staff'.

However, the problems did not go away and on October 22, 1957, the School Log reports:-

Dr. Reith, Mr. Forbes and two members of the City Architects Department visited the school to discuss the accommodation and future needs with the headmistress. It was proposed that an additional room - all purpose - with seating capacity for the whole school and a platform will be added in the playground. Official permission for this would have to be obtained.

Whether official permission was not granted is not noted, and even after a similar visit in the following year, life seemed to continue much as before at the school.

My children started at Blackhall School in 1963, when we came back from Berwickshire and they were in Primary 4 and 6. At that time there were only six classes because there was a 5/6 and a 6/7, of course that was the number of classroom they had, so they couldn't have any more. The old Horsa Huts were up then, I think they went up at the end of the war.

The school concerts were always in the church hall in Miss Forrest's day and Mrs. Malcolm's time and then we had two at Broughton and one at Clermiston and then at the New School.....there was no where in the old school that we could do anything like that. Miss Forrest used to stand up and say she was fighting to get more huts put up and finally they put up that big one at the gate and that eased things a bit.

MRS. E. STUART

The various huts which were in use prior to the new school being built

In spite of all these difficulties, the school continued to receive good reports from the education department. The curriculum became more wide ranging with visiting teachers for music, physical education and religion, plus many missionaries and temperance speakers. There were also visits to the Royal Scottish Museum, Lauriston Castle, the ballet, cinema and nature rambles. Perhaps the winters were colder in the early years of this century as there were quite a number of half days given for skating and sledging. Royal occasions were also marked by holidays and special events - some of the pupils attending a Youth Rally at Murrayfield in 1937 in the presence of King George and Queen Elizabeth and their daughters. In 1953 Blackhall Co-ordinating Committee presented the school with a Union Jack and Flag-staff to mark the Coronation and the flower beds at the gate were laid out in appropriate colours. Gardening appears to have featured quite frequently at the school, but of a changing nature as the school log and reminicences show.

SCHOOL LOG 1917
March 30 - Garden dug. Potatoes planted.
May 4 - Garden crops now in except for onions and leeks.

(1930's) All the activities were in the school but as you went in the gate, to the left by the railings there was a big cultivated area, where we used to keep gardens and we used to plant various things and take great pride in looking after our gardens and seeing whose came up best. And Miss Aitken used to come out and pass comments and tell you who was awarded the prize for the best kept garden.

MR. R. BOYCE

School Log 1947

October 10 - Bulbs - hyacinth, tulip, daffodil, narcissus, crocus and snowdrops, bought with part of the proceeds of the sale in June were planted during the week.

1954

February 25 - This is Arbor Day in Blackhall School. All week thoughts of trees have been introduced in every possible way in school work. This afternoon ten young flowering cherry trees were planted in the playground by twenty pupils, representatives of all classes in school. Councillor Colonel Drummond, Councillor Ingham, Mr. Harrison, the City Gardener, the Rev. R.J.W. Mathewson, among the visitors and many parents who attended the ceremony.

Just some of the cherry trees which surrounded the school

Some activities have changed a little but not that much.

When I first started teaching at Blackhall in 1969, the children went to Sciennes for swimming and they went by themselves.....changed days....it was usually the Primary 7 Class. Then they started going to Glenogle and people had to go with them, you couldn't leave them to go on their own now.

There was no gymn, so you had to clear the classroom to do movement to music and things like that. I remember an article in the press about Blackhall having to have School Dinners in the corridor, but, mind you it was a big corridor and nobody ever thought anything about it, it was as big as some rooms.

MRS. E. STUART

One such article appeared in the 'Evening News' in 1966, but it was 1971 before any further accommodation was erected, and once more it was in the form of classroom huts. This meant that Prize Givings and other occasions involving the whole school still had to be held elsewhere or were dependent on the vagaries of the Scottish climate.

> *I can remember having a Prize Giving out in the playground with the table out there and Mrs. Malcom was always keen that whoever was presenting the prizes wore a hat. And actually when I started teaching and we went to church at the end of term, all the teachers wore hats. I remember Mrs. Malcolm also liked the children to stand up when she came into the room and say 'Good morning, Mrs. Malcolm.' but I think she was the last Head to expect that.*
>
> *Mrs. Malcolm had the idea that they should pull down the Horsa Huts and build a two storey building with a gymn and still have the school in the middle of the catchment area, however that didn't come off. There was no P.T.A. in the early days, it was only during her time that it gradually came into being, but I think it has gone from strength to strength and it has done a lot of good. I remember there was a lot of pressing and campaigning to get the new school.*
>
> MRS. E. STUART

However, when plans for the new school in Craigcrook Road were eventually drawn up in 1976, the School Log reported that:-

> *The parents were shown plans of the new school and open plan teaching explained to them. Not everyone was happy over this idea. Staff were somewhat worried also. P.A. Committee Secretary and Chairman decided to write formally to the Department of Education.*

The 'New' Blackhall Primary School

But the plans were not altered and on Tuesday, the 19th of June, 1979 the new Blackhall Primary School was officially opened by Councillor Malcolm Knox. In the School Magazine produced 10 years later, there were accounts of the removal from the old school plus the 'teething problems' in the new.

After much campaigning by parents for a new school, it was finally announced in 1977 that one would be built in Craigcrook Road. More than two years passed before the school was ready for occupation but during that time a great deal of planning was done. Mrs. Malcolm retired in summer 1977 and Mrs. Walker became Headteacher. In the early months of 1979 the staff had several visits to the school to be shown the layout. The summer term of 1979 was a very busy one. All the cupboards, desks and drawers had to be emptied and the materials packed in cardboard boxes. It was a great opportunity to disperse with all the rubbish both generally and personally. Finally on June 1st we said good-bye to the old school. The children were given two days holiday - the Monday and the Tuesday but the staff reported to the new school on Monday June 4th to unpack and prepare the teaching areas for the children arriving on Wednesday June 6th, There was great excitement and everything was very strange. We had come from a school 75 years old with individual classrooms and huts in the playground to this brand new building with no doors, with wide open spaces and a gymn hall. At first both pupils and staff got a bit lost and were apt to turn the wrong way but very soon things settled down for the last few weeks of term and everything was in order for the start of the new term in August.

MRS. BETTY STUART, former teacher.

In the old school some of the radiators were inside cupboards so the children went into the cupboards to keep warm. When we moved to the new school a lot of books and maps were left behind because they were out of date. Anything that was worthwhile was put on trucks and driven to the new school. At first there were some problems with crowded cloakrooms, this was because Primary Seven had two classes which meant about 63 children. The solution was to have two separate bells, one class would go out and come in on the first bell and the other did the same on the second. When we first started teaching at the new school we found it difficult because there was another teacher's voice in the same area and it was difficult to concentrate. This was sorted out by one class doing something quiet while the other class was being taught and vice versa.

MISS MACKAY interviewed by Scott Mitchell and Stuart Masterton.

And there were other more dangerous problems. Initially there was only an unmade pavement part of the way from Ravelston Dykes Road to the school and in wet weather it 'became a quagmire, forcing youngsters to walk on the busy Craigcrook Road', as the Evening News reported on April 17th, 1980. This problem was eventually sorted out, only to be replaced by the perennial problem of the continually rising school roll causing accommodation difficulties. It is estimated that there will be 309 children on the Roll by August 1994 and a double transportable unit is likely to be in situ for the new intake then. The School Board are continuing to press for a permanent extension, plus some nursery places.

However, judging by the 'Blackhall Rap' written by pupil Colin Perkinsin 1991, the children are nevertheless enjoying their school days.

> We are ace,
> We are cool,
> We all come from Blackhall School.
>
> If you ask a person where to go,
> They will always let you know,
> Blackhall is the place to be,
> Because you'll live next to you and me.
>
> We are ace,
> We are cool,
> We all come from Blackhall School.

But what of the old School Building? It was demolished in 1989 to make way for the Queen's Court Retirement Housing and Miss E. Denholm sums up the feelings of many of the former pupils.

> *It was very sad to see the building coming down, I don't know why they couldn't have enlarged it, they could have built on to it rather than destroy it.*

Queen's Court Retirement Houses

PEOPLE

However, a village is not composed solely of buildings, what a village becomes is very much determined by its inhabitants and what they consider to be important. Blackhall has been fortunate in its past residents for they have all worked hard in their different ways to make the area a pleasant place in which to live. When asked, our present older residents recalled many names - Russell Paton, Sandy Forbes, David Mathewson the chemist, John Calder of Buchanan & Calder, Baillie Poole, Bella Beatson, Baillie Nelson, Miss Wilson the ironmonger and many, many more. Some names, however, cropped up so frequently that it seems only fitting to make a record of them.

Dr. Sutherland was up at the top of Blackhall, opposite where the Post Office is now, the big house there.

MRS. M. EDINGTON

He was a great old soul, you went and you saw him "Well, it's 'flue or something, go to your bed and I'll come and see you" and if he didn't come you just got up when you felt like it and if he came you knew you were awfully ill. Never came back if he didn't have to, so you just sort of got up when you felt like it. Oh he was nice.

MISS E. DENHOLM

I remember our doctor, Dr. Sutherland, he really was the typical good old family doctor. He was very very good to my father - he used to take him out on his rounds occasionally, my father wasn't able to drive or walk much.

MRS. A. C.

The local policeman was another who was liked and respected, but his police station/home was also a point of conjecture in the village - but the question as to whether it contained a cell or not can now be answered.

In line with Wood's house at Maidencraig there was a six foot wide row of causies across the road, which marked the boundary of Midlothian and the City of Edinburgh. The City policeman and our policeman used to meet there at certain times and sign each others books. The Police Station was the lodge into Ravelston House until Miss Murray Gartshore died and Mrs Stewart Clark bought the estate. The policeman then was Sandy Anderson and if he caught any of us young lads up to a bit of mischief or in places we shouldn't be, he would line us up and give us a skelp on the jaw and tell us not to do it again and if our folks got to hear about it, we got one on the other side to balance it up. If a policeman was doing that now he would be charged with assault. We always remained good friends with the policeman and in later years after he retired we used to visit him occasionally.

MR. R. RENTON.

Mr. Anderson, the policeman, in the police house in Marischal Place. He was a big solid man and made sure that the kids didn't get into much mischief.

MR. D. FRASER

Police Constable Watson

My father and family came to Blackhall in 1922. Dad replaced Sergeant Anderson, who flitted to a house above the last house opposite us. After that he built a house up at Blinkbonny on the side of Craigleith Station. It was the first new house up in that area.

Everyone seemed to quite like my Dad, the youngsters like my brother and myself had a great respect for him. I doubt if ever a youth went to court, he dealt with them himself - he was also the local Social Worker. In those days. we didn't have a Public House in Blackhall, but there were always a few drunks from time to time, I guess he just got them home if possible.

After Police Boxes came into fashion, Police Stations went up for sale to the highest bidder. Dad was fortunate he could buy his and his offer was accepted. Both my parents died there.

The people of Blackhall gave Dad a wallet of notes for a retiral present and the Police gave him a gold watch and chain and my mother got a gold watch. Both had their initials on it

MRS. M. KERR (NEE WATSON)

I remember climbing into Ravelston Estate over the wall and roaming around there with one eye open both for the Estate people and the local policeman, P.C. Watson or Cop Watson as we used to call him. He used to shoot there, I think he got permission to shoot, so there was a double reason for making sure we didn't mess about in there. We were never actually caught by him but there were times when we had to depart fairly hurriedly.

MR. A. MACDONALD.

The Police Office was near the Rec. They were nice friendly policemen and I think they cycled about if I remember correctly as well as the foot patrol...that was the old style when you had your local friendly bobby.

MRS. C. MITTELL

I remember Mr. Watson, he lived in Marischal Place and if he saw boys or anybody doing something they shouldn't, he would solemnly take down the names and addresses and then forget about it.

MISS M. MACDONALD

The house beside the Rec used to be the Police Station and it used to have the Board outside with folk wanted for different crimes and so forth. I heard it said that there was a cell attached to the house, but whether Jimmy Watson, ever had to use it I couldn't say - the worst he probably had to do was chase a lad after he'd broken a window with a ball or something. There was never crime as such in Blackhall. He was known by everybody, he was a big man was Jimmy Watson, he must have stood about 6 ft. 2 or 3 maybe more and he was a big barrel chested fellow too. And to me as a wee school boy he used to tower over you and intimidate you just by his presence, but he was very friendly nevertheless and he knew us all and chatted to us, and he was in and out the shops. I was probably at secondary school when Jimmy Watson retired as the policeman.

MR. R. BOYCE

The Police house had no cells. We used to stand on a stool at the kitchen window and watch Dad's 'captures' being guarded by our lovely chocolate curly haired retriever dog 'Rover', whilst they awaited the arrival of the Black Maria, which took them to the big West End Police Station. Needless to say we didn't see many in those days.

MRS. M. KERR (nee WATSON)

Another gentleman who was known by his occupation, but remembered by so many people in so many different ways, was **William Scott**, the local scavenger but known affectionately by everyone as Scottie the Scaffie. His work extended far beyond street cleaning and his small garden in Keith Row was a local attraction and his 'magic' tricks mystified the children.

Mr William Scott

He was a very likeable man and there was a marvellous story my father used to tell - that somebody thought they would play a joke on Scottie and they filled their bucket up with stones and the poor man couldn't even lift it, so he rang the bell and said 'Whae dae ye think I am, Samson?"

MISS M. MACDONALD

He was a character was Scottie. People used to always stop and look at his garden, it was a sort of a rockery and he would pick up anything in the street and put on this rockery - it was very artistically done. He was a nice wee man...used to wear his cap back to front for some reason.

MISS M. LONIE

When we were wee boys we used to go and see his rockery because it changed every day - sometimes he had ornaments in and he had lamps and bits of this and that.

MR. W. WOOD.

He was also a Baptist, he was a member of Charlotte Chapel, a very religious man and deeply involved and he used to go round singing his Baptist hymns while he was doing his work, you could hear him coming along.

MR. R. BOYCE

Scottie was also 'Leerie-licht-the-lamps' and was always welcome at our lamp at which we would gather to watch proceedings and be chatty. Sometimes he would show us his trick with a dice which we could never fathom. He held the dice between two fingers showing one side then the opposite one. Twice he would do this, then the third time when he turned it over the number on the face would mysteriously be different. "The quickness of the hand deceiving the eye," he said. Scottie would also be obliging to householders by looking after their poultry when they were away on holiday. His pride and joy was his front garden in Keith Row.

ANON

I remember him coming up to my father with a barrowload of manure for the garden and after he had unloaded it, he turned to where I was watching and he put a penny on his shovel and twirled the shovel round and kept the penny on it - and he said 'if you can do that you can keep the penny' but I never did it. It was a heavy shovel and I was a wee chap at the time.....

MR. A. MACDONALD

We used to have a concert in the Rec every year and he used to do a trick with burning newspapers and he balanced them in some way, I don't quite know how, on the end of his nose. He used to do it every year.

MR. W. WOOD

Another gentleman who had a great impact on the community, not through his occupation, but through all his voluntary work and hobbies, plus the strength of his personality was **George Nesbit.**

Mr George Nesbit

He lived in Craigcrook Road and as a small child, I called him the bee man, because he kept bees in his garden - his neighbours used to say laughingly that they were told to grow certain flowers for George's bees. He and my father both worked in Register House. George was the treasurer of the church and what he said went. You thought of the minister and then you thought of George. He was an important personage.

MRS. M. EDINGTON

He was an old neighbour of mine and a very familiar figure in Blackhall and an elder in St. Columba's for many years. I have a photograph of him planting Blackhall's Coronation tree in the park in Craigcrook Road. A memory I have of him is when

*stung by a bee from his own hives, he just flicked it off and said 'that one stung me'.
Never gave it another thought.*

MISS J. HOUGH
(Blackhall Bulletin 1982)

*He was a very tall man, he must have stood about six foot three in his prime, he was
well into his eighties when he died. When he was in church, he used to sit in the gallery
because he always went down to open the doors before the end of the service - he
regarded that as his job. He was church treasurer for goodness knows how long. He
always knew me as Robert, because he was my Sunday School teacher and then he was
superintendant at the Sunday School when I was still in it. They used to talk about
him jokingly as the 'Provost of Blackhall'.*

MR. R. BOYCE

*He was our Superintendant at the Sunday School....as wee boys we used to call him
Nisser. A big tall slow moving man, a gentle sort of chap - he put up with a terrible
lot from us little devils in the Sunday School - he was a nice type.*

MR. W. WOOD

*He was one of the leaders of the Sunday School - I remember a Sunday School party
where we had the usual tea and buns and towards the end of the tea, George Nesbit
was striding down majestically with a tray full of cups and saucers and some of us
lobbed buns into the middle of this tray and sploshed slops of tea up into his face. He
was such an imposing figure - a real character.*

*It was only after the war, when I was on to the Congregational Board etc that I really
got to know George - he never took 'No' for an answer, he'd stand at the door of the
church and button-hole you. I was Clerk to the Board when he resigned as Treasurer.
I got a phone call quite early in the morning saying "Come down and see me" so I went
down that evening and he said "I'm resigning as Treasurer and Convenor of the
Finance Committee." He was well up by then, and he said "I'm giving up everything
except the Bowling Club, it was the first treasurership I took on, so I want to keep it."
Then he said "But I'm only giving it up on condition that Pat Campbell is made the
Treasurer" Pat Campbell was Assistant Treasurer then and I said "Well, is he willing
to take it?" "Oh yes, he'll take it, I've told him."....that was his style.*

MR. A. MACDONALD

*He was treasurer of practically everything in the village. He was a kindly man, I don't
remember being frightened of him or anything like that, but he was a very erect and
I think he had rather a pauky sense of humour. My father knew him well.*

MISS M. MACDONALD

*He was a great man, Mr. Nesbit. I would say to him 'Now don't you come back.' He
was a great one for Flags....our front door - you had a glass door, then you had a front
door in two halves....and I would be away out and when I came back, here's a basket
of flags and a tin sitting and I would tell his daughter to tell him I'm no doing the
flags any longer....she was a very quiet soul, and she would say 'He'll not pay any
attention to me'.*

MRS. H. STURGEON

The Denholm Family 1909
Back Row from left to right: Henry Edgar, Margaret Scott, Matthew, Alexander Scott Junior,
Agnes Henderson and Charles Proctor
Front Row: Elizabeth Proctor, Alexander, Elizabeth (nee Purves) and William Purves.

One family with long standing connections in Blackhall are the **Denholms**. In the early 1850's, Matthew Denholm, moved with his family from Swanston Farm to Dean Park Farm, where he later became farm steward to the Gibson family. Dean Park Farm was situated about halfway up the present Queensferry Terrace, just below Ravelston Dykes, with fields running towards Blinkbonny.

In 1865, their son Alexander, aged 21 and a Master Blacksmith, followed his elder brother Thomas (a wheelwright) to Blackhall where he took over the village smithy. In the 1865 photograph of the village (See page 2), the man in the pony trap to the left of the picture is Matthew Denholm, while the figure standing by the cart in white apron and sleeves is his son Thomas. The village smiddy was where the Murray Gartshore Hall was built some 20 years later.

In 1872 the two brothers set up together in a Van Builders' business in Stockbridge, but returned to the village in 1876. By 1881 Alexander owned three houses known as 'Denholm Cottages' - the first with four rooms was occupied by James C. Simpson of Simpson's Dairy. He was known universally as J.C. with the first initial pronounced to rhyme with "high". Alexander with his wife and six children occupied the second cottage, which had three rooms' and the third was occupied by Charles Chambers and his family, an Englishman who was the Garrison Armourer at Edinburgh Castle.

In 1886 Alexander and his family left the village for a three year spell as by this time he was now in business for himself at Gilmore Park. He was now a widower and, through being an elder and precentor at Dean Free Church, met his second wife. It was also during this spell that he occasionally took the Dean F.C. choir to Blackhall to perform in the Gartshore Memorial Hall as recorded by his son Alexander Scott Denholm Jnr in his article in the 1918 edition of the Rec magazine - the same literary gentleman wrote the lengthy poem "A Blackhall Bowling Ballad."

In 1889, Alexander returned to Blackhall and joined Cramond Free Church (now Davidson's Mains Parish Church) and a year later became an elder there with a district comprising of 'Blackhall, Craigcrook, House o' Hill and Marchfield'.

In 1893, Denholm Cottage, a substantial, two storey stone building with slate roof, was built (see page 56 for photograph). It was in this house that his daughter Agnes Henderson recalled helping her mother - "All the boys had wooden kists beside their beds to keep their things in and in the evenings when they returned from work they had porridge. The bowls were set out on the window sill to cool and as they arrived from the station each one picked up his bowl, then ate his porridge in the kitchen before going to wash." His son William Purves remembers it as the place where he kept pigeons and rabbits in hutches behind the house.

In the 1890's Cramond Free Church formed a Band of Hope (Temperance Society) in Blackhall and the Kirk Session minutes report a membership of 65. Alexander was elected precentor at Cramond, but resigned in 1902 to join St. Columba's, where he later became an elder. In 1903 he became President of the Young Men's Guild, a position which he held until his death in 1911.

About 1904, Alexander had Denholm Cottage demolished and replaced by numbers 9-17 Marischal Place, which included a number of shops. While the building was taking place, the family moved to Hillview Terrace and when it was completed, they moved into 17 Marischal Place which became the family home. The date of completion '1905' is engraved on a plaque the side of 13 Marischal Place facing Craigcrook Place and Alexander's initials are engraved on another plaque facing Queensferry Road. No 17, which Alexander still called Denholm Cottage, had a wash house on the ground level entered from a side garden and Elizabeth Vance's daughter recalls her mother telling her that it was equipped with what sounds like one of the first 'washing machines' - a handle being turned to operate wooden paddles. While any of the sons were at home, on returning from work they entered the house via the wash house, cleaned up and only then went up the back stairs. Alexander entered by the front door regardless. His wife was a gentle woman with a reputation for kindness and the people in Blackhall village came to her for help in numerous ways; the Denholm family Christening robes being lent out to lots of new babies in the village. As an older man, he did not like to be kept up beyond what he considered to be his bedtime. Should the company be lingering beyond what he felt to be a reasonable hour, he would arise, announce "Well, it's time all good people were in their beds" and take himself off.

In 1909-10, Alexander moved his business to Washington Lane, Dalry and by that time he was employing about twenty men including four of his sons - Matthew as office manager, Henry as carpenter, Alexander junior as blacksmith and Charles as a painter. Those who lived in Blackhall travelled daily to and from their work by train from Craigleith Station to Dalry. Two of Alexander Denholm's grand-daughters Eileen and Mary still live in Marischal Place and their brother **Bill**, who supplied all the above information, now lives in Harpenden but still takes a keen interest in Blackhall

It would not be right to complete this chapter without making mention again of **Miss Murray Gartshore**, who did so much, albeit in a proprietorial fashion, to supply the grounds and facilities for the villagers to fulfil their ambitious schemes. Just how much she did will be seen more fully in the next chapter.

CHAPTER 10

LEISURE ACTIVITIES

As has been seen in previous chapters, between the quarries and the farms and their own vivid imaginations, the children of the area had no problems about entertaining themselves.

However, organised events were not ignored and one day in June each year has continued through the decades to bring children to Ravelston Park - namely the Blackhall Sports Day. Exactly when the Sports were inaugurated has been impossible to establish definitely but it seems likely that it was around 1909-10 shortly after the Recreational Association came into being. Certainly the Sports hold memories for a great number of Blackhall's residents.

It was the big event of the year and was organised by the Rec. A brass band always played at the Sports - they sat on chairs.

MISS M. MILLER.

They had the Blind Band from Edinburgh and they used to meet at Craigleith Station and Nellie Landels used to ride on this big horse out in front and everybody else followed on behind right along to the Park. The band was all joined together so that they could all turn at the one time. They sat in a circle in the park and they played all afternoon - classical music, really nice music.

In the marquee you could get a bottle of lemonade for tuppence and ha'penny cones. You had your tinny, I hated those tinnies because I hate hot tea, I like it so that I can drink it. They had all the races - it was a great day and they always got good weather. If it didn't turn out a good day, it was to be held in the church hall, but I never remember it ever being held in the church hall. It was always some time in June - and it used to go on till about seven o'clock at night and you were all dressed up in your best shorts and shirt and rubber shoes.

MR. H. ERSKINE

The Blackhall School children took part in the procession but the Merchant Company and such like children didn't consider that they should take part. Then there were ponies and traps with various people in them and Nan Landells used to ride this horse up at the head. Then there were pony rides in the park and all the usual sports. I remember watching the ladies slaving over coal fires and boiling up tea.

MR. A. MACDONALD

There was a Mr. Goodall stayed in Keith Crescent and he had a grain merchant's place at Leith, so he used to bring up his horse - and my father had a wee governess cart....and the kids used to get hurls in it on the Sports Day.

MISS B. DUNCAN

Blackhall Sports was one of the highlights of our year. We just had races and very nice prizes. There was always a champion and they were idolised when we were wee. They really had very good prizes, I think Mary, my sister, once won a watch.

MISS E. DENHOLM

An Early Sports Day

Somebody used to come and throw out great handfuls of sweets and then when we were coming out we were all given an orange and wicked people like my older brothers used to go along and climb the wall and go back in again.

MISS M. MACDONALD

The field which is now the park belonged to Ravelston and the ladies of Ravelston House used to allow them to use it for the Blackhall Sports. I couldn't really tell you exactly when they started but I do remember them well and I was only what ten or eleven when I left there (1920) so they must have been going for a few years before then. Of course it was The Rec that organised the sports. They made the tea on the fires and they put up tents, it was often very wet - it was quite a day. Now my father was always very interested, but he didn't believe in having gala queens and that kind of thing, he thought that wasn't right because it sort of picked out one person who was prominent but they have always kept it to the sports, and I think he would be very pleased to know that it still keeps to that.

MRS. C. MITTELL

A Later Sports Day around 1968-70

The Church also organised many activites for the young people.

Naturally among the first organisations to be formed were the SUNDAY SCHOOL and the JUNIOR CHOIR

A Christmas Party in the Old Hall

The Primary Sunday School was in the afternoon at one stage and the older ones went after church, from about half past twelve to half past one. Then some people made the excuse that they didn't go to Sunday School because their mother had the lunch ready, so it was changed and for a while they had it before church. The boys sat on one side and the girls on the other, you didn't have mixed classes

MRS. M. EDINGTON

The Sunday School was quite big. I remember at the Harvest Thanksgiving, we used to gather in the old wooden hall and the Church Officer was ringing the bell before we went into church - I miss the church bell.

ANON

I went through the Sunday School and then into the Fellowship. We used to give parties for the poorer children from the Canongate at Christmas time. The Youth Fellowship used to bring so many of them out and we gave them a party - that was in the old hall.

ANON

A Kinderspiel

A KINDERSPIEL given in St. Columba's old church hall probably in 1916. It is perhaps curious that the German word kinderspiel was retained for juvenile plays of this kind at a time when Scott-Lyon's German buns became Belgian buns at the outbreak of war. At the time the minister was Mr. Baird, who can be seen on the right.

The organist who produced the show is on his right (partly hidden). The kinderspiel performed was "The Princess in Poppyland" and the plot had to do with the villanous Baron Insomnia stealing sleep from the unfortunate subjects until the hero foiled his wicked plans and won the hand of the princess.

MR. D.FRASER
(Blackhall Bulletin 1984)

I remember being taken when I was quite young by my mother to what I think was the old fashioned type of kinderspiel in the church hall but I would have been quite young at the time.

MISS M. MCDONALD

Mr. Cunningham, who had the fruit shop where the T.S.B. is now, ran the Junior Choir, I think he was the organist as well. The Junior Choir always sang for the evening service.

MRS. M. EDINGTON

And there was a Mr. Cunningham who used to play the organ in the church and he organised children's shows, the Kinderspiel - all the youngster were in it.

ANON

1990's Junior Choir being conducted by Jeanette Lowrie

Another organisation with very early beginnings in the area was THE BOYS' BRIGADE COMPANY. In the Congregational Supplement of May, 1901, is the following report:-

Our own little company has made an excellent start. We were most fortunate in obtaining the services of Sergeant Major Fraser as a drill instructor. The Company is the 29th Edinburgh and has already taken part in several of the services and special parades of the Battalion. Our esteemed member and elder Mr. John Sturrock has promised a silver medal to the boy of the 29th Company, who in the opinion of the officers shall most deserve it.

However, a further report in October, 1905, shows that it was a somewhat different Boys' Brigade to that of to-day.

The new session of the Boys' Brigade has opened most auspiciously with a membership of 32. Mr. Robertson has again kindly agreed to act as instructor. As several of the original guns had gone missing and others were a good deal the worse for wear, we have purchased twenty carbines from the War Office, which have been distributed to the older boys in the company and have given great satisfaction.

St. Columba's no longer has a B.B. Company, but local resident **Mr. R. Boyce** recalls his days in 29th Company of the Boys Brigade

I joined the Life Boys in 1928 and went into the Brigade in 1931. The Company strength was around 30 at that time and I remember the next four years as a very happy time featuring Drill Parades, gymnastics, ambulance classes, swimming, football matches in the winter and cricket and athletics in the summer plus, of course, the summer camps. As 1933 was the B. B.'s Jubilee Year, there was no camp and the whole company participated in a Review on 9th September. Over 30,000 officers and boys paraded in the Queen's Park, Glasgow before Prince George, later Duke of Kent, and this was followed by a Conventicle on the Sunday at Hampden. Sadly it was that same year that the B.B. company ceased to exist in Blackhall.

The reason for the demise of the Boys' Brigade Company is to be found in the Church Supplement of the same year

Owing to the recent decision of the Kirk Session to start a Scout Group in connection with our church, the officers, after careful consideration, have tendered their resignations as from the end of the current session, 30th September, 1933. This decision was made primarily on the grounds that in the opinion of the officers, based on the recruiting statistics of the past few years, there are not at present sufficient boys in the district to support two virile organisations, and secondly, that it is not in the best interests of the boys to have two similar organisations running side by side.

Prior to this date, THE SCOUTS in the area appear to have met in a variety of places as the following shows:-

When I joined the Wolf Cubs, we met in Simpson's Dairy in the barn. I remember Bill Stalker was the Cub Master and he was a disabled man and went around in a wheel chair.

MR. D. FRASER

I was in the Scouts and the Scouts had a hall from my Uncle Jim (Simpson's Dairy), that had been a byre at one time, but they converted it into a hall.

MR. H. ERSKINE

A Scout Camp in 1934

I was in the Davidson's Mains Scouts, because when I got to the Scout stage there were no Scouts at Blackhall, it was the B.B.s. There had been Scouts apparently but I didn't know that until they resurrected them. A few years after I joined Davidson's Mains they reformed the Blackhall troop, because I remember we were highly indignant at one or two boys, who lived in Blackhall who left Davidson's Mains Scouts to go to Blackhall Scouts and we felt they were a bit traitorous. I remember the Boys' Brigade use to meet in the church hall - the Scouts when they restarted, they met in Forrest's Farm (Craigcrook Farm) barn which maybe implied that the Boys' Brigade still had the church. Before they resurrected the Blackhall Scouts, we used to have three church parades a year - one to Cramond, one to Davidson's Mains and one to Blackhall. We used to have to go away up to Davidson's Mains and then marched all the way down again to Blackhall, flags flying and all the rest of it.

MR. A. MACDONALD

I had been in Davidson's Mains Scouts and Walter Davidson had the idea of starting Scouts in Blackhall, which have been continuous since then (about 1932) and we had our meetings in the loft of one of the barns at Craigcrook Farm and we were there for quite some time.

DR. A. ROSS

75 YEARS OF SCOUTING

During the 1983/84 year we are celebrating a double Jubilee - of our original foundation in 1909 (75 years ago) and of our rebirth in 1933 (50 years ago).

The Group was originally called the 53rd Edinburgh and was founded in 1909 by Mr. A.S. Nicolls, who led the boys. In 1910, Captain Dewar of Drylaw House became Scoutmaster and that summer led 30 boys back to Heriot Camp - "the wettest I can remember" was his subsequent comment. In 1911 the Group re-registered as the 23rd Midlothian which it remained until the mid 1970s. In those days the Group met at Drylaw House and flourished with summer camps and week-end trips. In 1912 a bugle bands was formed. Scout uniform cost 6/- and a whole week's camp 6/6 (32p!). Changed days, changed values. The outbreak of war in 1914 saw the immediate departure of leaders and older boys. The troop continued to meet largely run by PLs and latterly helped by William Stalker, a scouter who was confined to a wheel chair. At this time the meeting place was a cow byre, roughly where Henry's Pub (Capital Foods) now stands. By 1922, however, the troop had ceased to exist.

In 1933, the 23rd came to life again now sponsored by Blackhall Parish Church. The Scouts met in the "Scout Hall" Craigcrook Farm, while the cubs met in Blackhall Public School. The Rev. Fred. Sim was Group Scoutmaster while Mr. Thomas Jack and Miss Rita Green were Scout and Cub Masters respectively with 19 Scouts and 20 Cubs. In 1955 Stanley Vaughan became Scoutmaster and in the following eight years transformed the group in numbers and in scope of programmes. Camps became increasingly adventurous. "Flying High" the group show was first provided in 1958 and the group magazine was first published in 1960 and a printing press was acquired. Thanks to the generosity of Mr. Boland (the land-owner) and the hard work of the Parents' Committee the Scout Hut on Craigcrook Road was erected and opened in 1963.

In 1959 a third cub pack was formed and the troop was divided into two - "Craigcrook" meeting in the Church Hall and "Ravelston" at the new hut.

At the end of 1962 the group had 199 members - the then cub masters being Angus Troup, Patsy Brown and Maida Sims, the Scout Masters Stanley Vaughan and Bill Gauld, presided over by Bobby Bee the group scoutmaster. No one would deny that the group's moving spirit was Stanley.

In 1965 the Rovers Crew was reestablished with Ian Macgregor as leader. In 1967 Venture Scouting replaced Rovering as the senior section and the 23rd Venture Unit became an outstanding success. For a while it owned its own double decker bus, converted for luxurious living and went abroad in it. The unit's annual jumble sale has become a feature of the Blackhall Calendar.

In 1967 Jim Watters became Scout leader. The two troops were reunited and in succeeding years Jim has built up a team of assistant leaders and introduced a concensus style of leadership. The team of leaders has remained constant over eight years. The three cub packs, led by Helen Morton, Niall Kennedy and Pam Taylor, each have their individual but happy styles. The Venture Unit has Alastair Reid as its Scouter. Since 1978 this diverse but successful group has been co-ordinated by Ian Macgregor as group scout leader.

What is it all about? It's about helping boys grow up to be positive, responsible and

outward looking. Over the years the steady but unobtrusive support of St. Columba's
Church and its ministers has helped to point the direction.

Now in our Jubilee year, we have 190 members, but it all depends on individuals
prepared to share the vision and give generously of themselves. We have such people
and, I believe, the support of the community. May it ever be so.

I.G.S.M.
(Blackhall Bulletin 1984)

In 1992 the Scouts presented a cheque for £1,523 to the
Western General Hospital Oncology Department in memory of Jim Watters

An organisation for girls also started in 1901, but went under the rather daunting
title of GIRLS' WORK PARTY and it seems that the girls were taught sewing and
dressmaking. In 1912 it changed its name to Girls' Work Party and Drill, when a class
for 'physical drill and Swedish exercise' was included. There were 42 names on the roll
and an average attendance of 36. Two competitions had been held during the session,
one for doll dressing and one for plain sewing. In July 1915, the following report
appear in the Church Supplement:-

The girls who had regularly attended the Blackhall Work Party during the winter
wished to form a JUNIOR GUILD. Accordingly a meeting was called when their
desire was agreed to.

It was decided to hold a Sewing Meeting once a week on Friday during the winter
and occasionally a musical evening when tea would be served.

In 1930 the name was changed to GIRLS' ASSOCIATION and the slightly lighter note of a Hallowe'en party introduced.

The 202nd Guides held a Reunion in 1993 to celebrate their 50th birthday

The 202nd Company of GIRL GUIDES was formed in September, 1933 under the guidance of Miss A. Mathewson, daughter of the local chemist and Session Clerk of that time. And the following year a Brownie Pack came into being.

> *I was in the Brownies - I think my big sister was the first sixer in the Brownies, they must just have started not all that long prior to the war maybe about 1935 or 6, something like that.*
>
> MRS. M. EDINGTON

> *And they started up a Guide movement and I was one of the first people in the Guides and they met originally in the old Blackhall School. I enjoyed the Guides very much, it was a good crowd and I still know some of them and see them.*
>
> MISS M. MACDONALD

One of the later organisations to be formed for young people was the YOUTH FELLOWSHIP. According to the Church Supplement of September, 1948, it was formed then to 'fill a serious gap in St. Columba's activities' as the article went on to explain thus:-

> *Entering into full Church membership or preparing to do so, besides awakening young people to their spiritual responsiblities, brings with it a desire to be doing something as*

proof of their sincerity in the vows they have made. This desire leads some to be Rovers, others to be Rangers, and a few brave souls to teach in the Sunday School. It still leaves in a vacuum of inactivity, those perfectly normal people who feel no urge to 'rove', 'range' or 'teach'. Yet this less extrovert group may have a very vital contribution to make to the life of the church. With this problem in mind then, the idea of a Fellowship was mooted, and a provisional committee elected to get it started during May and June.

Membership of the fellowship was open to all those between eighteen and thirty five. The programme included discussions, talks given by invited speakers, Bible Study and joint meetings with neighbouring Fellowships.

There is no longer a Fellowship at St. Columba's with such a wide age range, Grassroots meeting only part of the need expressed, but forty years later a Reunion of former members was held with over one hundred former members and their wives/ husbands present.

Surely a sign that it had been very much a fellowship! **Margaret Edington** recalls those early days.

The Youth Fellowship started when we were seventeen. We had just joined the church, Mr. Matheson was the minister then, and we had been attending the Communicants' Class all winter and there were 26 of us in it. We had nearly all gone through Sunday School and Bible Class together and we joined the church in the February. After about six months, we began to feel 'Well, who are we and what do we do now?' and Muriel Morton and I went to Mr. Matheson and said 'Do you think we could start a Youth Fellowship? And he said 'Oh yes, I've just been waiting for you to come and ask.' And years later I thought how wise he was If he had said to us the week after we joined the Church 'Now we're going to start the Youth Fellowship', we probably wouldn't have been interested, but he let us feel that break, that feeling of wanting something as a group together and it was a very successful Youth Fellowship. For many years we took services at the Royal Infirmary on a Sunday morning. Now we had to walk there and it needed a minimum of six, but was better with eight. We did it in rotation, so maybe your turn came round once a month or something like that. The more able ones took turns to prepare and the rest were just the back up with the singing and there had to be a pianist in the group. The patients seemed to appreciate it, we always went to the same ward and after the service we went round and chatted to them. We used to go down to a home in Ferry Road for old ladies - it seemed a dark and dismal place. We used to go at Christmas time and sing carols to them and again go round and talk to them.

There was and is certainly no shortage of associations or clubs in Blackhall for adults to join, indeed too many to do any real justice to in this chapter, but hopefully most will be touched upon.

Early Days of the Blackhall Bowling Club

As previously mentioned, the BLACKHALL BOWLING CLUB was formed in 1898 and has gone from strength to strength. An excellent booklet entitled "No End" has been written by Mr. J B Barclay on its history, so only a little will be written here. The Green was originally on the site now occupied by the Tennis Club and moved to its present site in 1913. The membership is limited to 120 men, 55 ladies and 16 juniors. Many trophies and cups have been won by the club and it had the reputation for combining a high standard of play with a friendly and pleasant atmosphere, some of which is captured in the last verse of A S Denholm's marathon poem of 35 verses written during the First World War.

> And may we lang w' health be spared
> Till age the hert blood cools,
> Tae meet the gether and enjoy
> A guid game at the bools.

The ground for the Bowling Club was let from Miss Murray Gartshore, and it was in the hall built by that same lady in memory of her father that the RECREATIONAL ASSOCIATION was formed in 1908.

It has already been mentioned that the Murray Gartshore Hall served Blackhall as a church, school, lending library and bank, but for many it was simply the home of 'The Rec'.

The Murray Gartshore Hall is on the left of the picture beside the lampost

If you look closely at the face of the Recreational Hall building, you'll see the top of a stone tablet with a fancy bit at the top - it's submerged below the wooden strip with the Insurance Agent's name on it - but on that tablet there's a date and I've a feeling that there's something about the Murray Gartshore Hall as well, but it's been covered up for such a long time, well over twenty years. The Recreation Club used to have an illuminated sign hanging outside the door.....it was a red neon sign - Blackhall Recreation Association.

MR. R. BOYCE

My father went to the Rec a lot and played billiards and, of course, females were not allowed there really, except when they had any concerts, we used to go and attend them

MRS. C. MITTELL

The Rec was a great place at that time and there were an awful lot of members of the Rec - 5 shillings a year.....I used to say to my mother, 'I need 5 shillings for the Rec due on so-and-so, is there anything you want done?' and she used to find things for me to do because she thought it was a good thing, the Rec. They used to run concerts and that; Scottie the Scaffie used to balance a lighted paper on his nose, we had good nights in it. Now they had a very successful Billiard Team - Walter Park and Jock Paterson were two of the team - they went right through the season and won the final. There were three tables - the big table, the Match Table was through in the back room, and a big table and small table in the front - that's where you learnt to play the game, and through from there was the domino room, never cards. Bob Forbes looked after the tables, he ironed them and kept them clean and match fit.

MR. H. ERSKINE

There were two brothers prominent in Blackhall when I was young. There was Forbes the builder and Bob Forbes the joiner and he stayed in the house above the Rec....he was a sort of caretaker, it was a sort of side job, he got the house in with it. They had a little museum up there - all bits and pieces connected with Blackhall - but it's all gone. Upstairs was the house and a little part of it was the museum and a library...you were able to borrow books.

MR. W. WOOD

As I got older my father and I used to go down to the Rec and play billiards. Snooker wasn't a fashionable thing in those days. There was a small library attached to the Rec but it was very very limited in its scope.

The only other thing connected with that was a Savings Group - a Penny Bank - with the famous George Nesbit....if there was anything connected with keeping track of money, George was doing it. He and I sat there on a Monday night and took in or gave out money. The money was put into the Savings Bank the next day and it only became a problem in November, when the interest came due because the money was being put in and taken out week in, week out and we had to do everything by calculating how much interest there was because they had taken out and how much to give them because they'd put some more in, that was a big job.

DR. A. ROSS

On a Monday night, the bell would ring at the Recreational Hall and you would go with your pennies and if you went with sixpence, oh boy, you were a millionaire...it was just pennies at that time really.

MISS B. DUNCAN

They did have some youngsters but it was mainly older men, my father used to go every night. The highlight of our life was the concert they had in the Rec every year and that was about all the entertainment there was in Blackhall...we used to have some real good times. There was a lending library in the Rec, we used to go there for books.

MISS E. DENHOLM

From November, 1909, the library lent out books at the modest charge of 1/-. a year. The present BLACKHALL LIBRARY building was opened in 1966, although books had been available from huts from 1947.

The Recreational Association continued to use the Murray Gartshore Hall until 1968, after which it was used as a small supermarket.

The Murray Gartshores also let the land for the RAVELSTON GOLF CLUB, which was incorporated as a limited company on the 11th October, 1912. The object of the club was 'to promote the game of golf or any other kind of amusement, sport or entertainment.' There were originally fourteen directors and the entrance fee was one guinea and an annual subscription of £1.11.6d. for men and one guinea for ladies. Now the club has 400 ordinary members, 150 ladies who have equal rights, and 100 five days members. There are no junior members, but youngsters can become full members at 16 and can be introduced as guests from the age of 12. There is a long waiting list.

The first directors of the Golf Club

Ravelston Golf Club was where we hammered ourselves to pieces. In those days the offices, the Insurance offices closed at half past four in the summer and we would get out and up to the golf course often by about five o'clock - you could be out from the town in less than ten minutes then - and we would play twenty seven holes in the evening. The first nine holes were clear, then the second we got away with the people who were coming on at the sort of normal evening rounds and by the time we played our third nine, they were on their second nine......there used to be an arrangement that the people starting on their first nine and the people starting on their second nine played alternately, but if we got away early, our first nine didn't count.

MR. A. MACDONALD

The Tennis Club

The BLACKHALL TENNIS CLUB was formed in 1915 on the site previously occupied by the Bowling Club and has continued to grow. A new clubhouse was erected in 1974 and the red blaes courts upgraded to all weather courts in 1976. Its membership now stands at 120 senior members and 110 junior members with a waiting lists for juniors.

There also appear to have been one or two football teams in the area. As previously mentioned, Mrs. Stewart Clark of Ravelston allowed the BLACKHALL ATHLETIC LADS to use Ravelston Park as their ground and provided them with a strip, and it is that team which stimulates most memories .

Willie Denholm and I ran the football team....Blackhall Athletic Lads. It was a very successful team - I think it started about 28 or 29....there was Davie Noble who moved on to higher things in football and Frankie Westwater moved on....it was a good team and there were selectors there picking them out, so, of course, we had to take in strangers for the sake of keeping the team going and it was still going, I think, in 38 or 39 or even maybe longer....

MR. H. ERSKINE

The Blackhall Athletic Lads used to play at one time up at where Craigleith Crescent is now, there was a field up there. The strip was black and white I remember and Sam Adams was their trainer.

MR. W. WOOD

Blackhall Athletic Lads

I used to play for the Blackhall Athletic Lads, but there was another team as well, I think they were known as the RAVELSTON ROVERS or something like that.

MR. A. BEWS.

There used to be a football club along at the Marle Pits, the MUIRHOUSE VIOLET FOOTBALL CLUB I think it was called.....that was more Davidson's Mains and then there was the Blackhall Athletic Lads.....my father took a great interest in that and of course David Noble went on to play for Clyde or somewhere.....my father William and his brother Matthew were both involved in it.

MISS E. DENHOLM

The BADMINTON CLUB was formed in 1912 but was disbanded again at the outbreak of war in 1914 and was not re-formed until 20th September, 1930, when it was said to have thirty three members and was proving to be very popular.

We had a very good Badminton Club at that time, we were the champions of Edinburgh never mind this district. I think it was on the go before the First War but, of course, it was stopped during the war, but it was revived and probably just as successful then as it was before.

DR. J. HARLAND

I played in the Badminton Club and that was certainly on the go Pre-war, and it had obviously been there for quite a while. It was in the old hall and the old hall didn't have that much space at the sides. We always used to laugh and say 'Oh they had to build the new halls because Bruce Jolly went through the floor at Badminton.

MRS. M. EDINGTON

However, there were also many less physical activities. St. Columba's CHURCH CHOIR came into being when the iron church was erected, and the congregation has been fortunate in having the worship led by many gifted choristers and organists over the years.

At one time there also appears to have been a BLACKHALL ORCHESTRA, but when it came into being and for how long it existed is not recorded.

The austerity of the war years brought about a renewed interest in recreational pursuits and several new association were formed.

The DRAMATIC CLUB actually came into being during the war raising money for Prisoners of War, and then for the new Church Hall, which was at that time in the planning stages.

The Drama Society - Mrs. Alexander put on a few plays in the old wooden hall.....the new hall was built in 1956.....she had been running it after the War in the late forties and then this chappie who was the assistant Scout Master and I put our noses into the Drama Club and said 'Look, why don't you let us make decent scenery for you'....so we made scenery for them and Mrs. Alexander did the first two I think and then she gave up. So we reconstituted a new Dramatic Society in 1949 and I've been the stage manager since then. It has no particular history but it's done very well - it's entered the One-act Play Festival of the Scottish Community Drama Association on three, I think, occasions......and we had five cups over that period. Since then we've not entered it,

A Drama Production of 'Cranford' in 1966

because it's terribly difficult when you're doing a play in March as we do, the first round in Edinburgh is in the end of January and the second round is end of February or something and you've got to keep the One Act Play hot and at the same time get on with your Three Act Play for here, which after all provides the money that keeps you going and allows you to enter because you have transport of scenery and everything when you go to these outside venues.

DR. A. ROSS

In October 1951 THE SCOTTISH COUNTRY DANCE CLUB was formed.

Dolly Flint, Margaret Bee and Chrissie Ritchie took on the task of forming the club. Mr. Antony was appointed treasurer and an enjoyable time was had by the members for the princely sum of an old sixpence per evening. Mr. and Mrs. McCann supplied the music, joined by Mr. Anderson on special occasion. The club was held in the old hall, where the danger of tripping over uneven boards was ever present. With the opening of the new hall, the club also had new teachers, Mrs. Hutchison, Mrs. Bennet and Mrs. Robertson.

MRS P. GORDON
(Blackhall Bulletin 1991)

The Club continues to flourish under the leadership of Pat Gordon and Sheila Milne.

In 1961 the OVER SIXTIES CLUB came into being and the large membership has enjoyed an interesting and varied programme over the years. Under its auspices, the ART CLUB was formed and its annual exhibition has given pleasure to the community.

The Over Sixties Club celebrate its 21st birthday in 1982

As with the youth organisations, there was some separation of the sexes. In 1903 the YOUNG MEN'S GUILD was formed and met in the Recreational Hall and the objects of the Association were to 'develope Christian character, promote Christian fellowship, the study of Scripture and the advancement of true religion'. The men took it in turns to lead the group discussions on topics such as 'Reasonableness in Prayer', 'Lessons from the Apostles'and 'Visions and Realities'. The Guild appeared to have disbanded some time after the First World War, possibly due to the number of young men lost in that war.

However, less that 30 years later, another BLACKHALL MEN'S GROUP was formed, due it seems to an article by J.T. in the Congregational News of July 1947 - part of which is featured below:-

> It has long seemed to the writer that we have throughout the years come to accept almost as Gospel many purely man-made rules and ordinances which have little to do with basic Christianity. It is difficult to particularise in a note such as this, but does it really matter which particular monies go to which funds, and when, or what forms of Sunday observance it might be desirable to enforce, as against making up our minds on such a problem as to whether it is right or wrong to kill our fellow men at stated periods? While it is not a new question to ask whether we can imagine Christ in a bombing plane or working a machine gun, it just has to be faced some time, and

churches have nothing to gain and everything to lose by continuing to sit on the fence - and apparently on each side of it too.

The main object of this note, however is to put forward the suggestion that some medium might be found in St. Columba's for the free discussion of this and other matters which vitally affect our whole community, and the vital task of living closer to each other and to the golden rule.

The writer has in mind the men of this congregation as we never seem to initiate or accomplish very much in unison. Do we men really know each other, apart from brief contacts on Sunday? Much real fellowship and practical Christianity was achieved not so long ago through the initial agency of a stirrup pump and bucket of water, but unfortunatelty we do not seem to have put anything in place of these useful articles or the spirit which they engendered.

Briefly the plea is for some form of men's meeting or guild (but please not a talking shop) to study and to serve in divers ways and to help knit closer the corporate life of our community.

The Group was formed in October 1947 and with the stated objectives being to:-

'hold meetings for the discussion of matters of interest, particularly with a view to the fostering of the Christian community spirit, the undertaking of projects of practical service suitable to the need of the neighbourhood, the stimulation of social and cultural interests and, generally, to promote neighbourliness by developing a sense of responsibility in the life and problems of the community.'

In 1952 a literary wing of the group carried out research and worked together in producing a history of Blackhall, which unfortunately was never published, but the original can be viewed in the Edinburgh Room at the Central Library, George IV Bridge.

Pat Easson was not a member of the original group but he does recall how they sought to carry out those objectives at a later date.

We did some one off jobs like helping to build the wooden hut at the Church adjacent to the 'tin hall' - it was a pre-fab surplus war stock; and erecting a flag pole at the old Blackhall School to commerate the Coronation, but most of the things we did were on a regular basis. We used to collect and repair toys and send them to the Pleasance Trust for distribution at Christmas time. Then we also collected vegetables from local gardens and allotments and delivered them to the Council of Social Services.

There was the weekly rota of members to help with the bathing of older boys at the Trefoil School, known as the Bath Parade and this we did for many years. We also had a transport rota for the handicapped or disabled.

At Christmas time we organised a pantomime trip for the under-privileged children in the Pleasance area, but the involvement we enjoyed most was the week long summer camps for boys from the Drylaw and Pleasance areas. The Group made the arrangements, provided the leaders, found the money etc. and we involved the community by making up the menus in advance, quantifying the non-perishable goods required, listing these in one lots and going round the doors asking people to supply one lot and deliver it to one of the garages.

As social conditions improved there didn't seem to be the same need for our services, and then I think the advent of T.V. took its toll, our members preferred to sit in the comfort of their easy chairs at home instead of the hard chairs at Blackhall School.

The Group was famous (or infamous) for its annual Burns Supper held at the Peacock Inn - in fact, I think it outlived the Group.

In the late 1980's yet another men's group was formed, namely the BLACKHALL PROBUS CLUB for retired business men. This proved to be so popular that a second Probus Club was formed and given the name CRAIGLEITH.

In November, 1905, a branch of the WOMAN'S GUILD was formed at St. Columba's and has carried out sterling work throughout the years, both locally and through the national movement.

My mother used to do all the cutting out of material for the Guild Sales of Work - Mrs. Sim used to call her the pyjama maker because my mother made pyjamas galore. Then they were stopped and they had collection boxes and I used to go up to the Guild and help to count the money - it was no trouble to me because I was working with money every day.

MRS. H. STURGEON

I was the Convenor of the Work Party at the Guild one winter and on the second Thursday of every month - I met up with the Home Mission Delegate of Cramond -

The Woman's Guild celebrate 80 years

and we went up to Glenlochart House and went round with the trolley and sold them whatever...it was the coupon time. And I remember I asked the matron if there was anything the Guild could do for them in the way of knitting and she said "Oh we could do with some knitted capes for the old folks - I could give you the wool."So I said we would and one day we were sitting having our lunch and a big van drove up at the gate and here was the wool for the capes - packets and packets and packets of it! However, I took it down to the Guild and told them what had happened and we got the capes all done that winter, the ladies were really very good. The matron at the home was most grateful. It was quite interesting going up there though and they got to know you - I think I did it for about seven years.

ANON

Another very practically minded group was the KNITTING CIRCLE, which was founded in 1952 as a 'Work Party for Refugees' and over the years sent out parcels to Cologne, Oldenburg, Austria, Tibetan refugees, Latvian families and Leper colonies in Calabar, Nepal and Biafra. Home needs were not forgotten either as parcels were sent to W.V.S, Old Folks Welfare and the Royal Victoria Hospital. The group ceased to exist in the 80's but has been replaced by the CRAFT GROUP, which works towards producing all manner of craft work for sale, with the money going towards specific charities.

Another active group is the SCOTTISH WOMEN'S RURAL INSTITUTE

There was a big Rural here, at one time we were 250 strong and we met in Davidson's Mains in a big hall - it belonged to Cramond Kirk and we got it quite cheap and, of course, it was sold and then we had an awful job - we met in a wee hut for a while, then we met in the Episcopal church hall.

MRS. H. STURGEON

The Rural now meets in St. Columba's Hall, as does TUESDAY TOPICS, the FLOWER CLUB, the MOTHER and TODDLER GROUP and the PLAYGROUP.

The BLACKHALL CO-ORDINATING COMMITTEE was formed on December 8th, 1949 with the aim of co-ordinating existing organisations and fostering and developing a community spirit through recreation, social and educational interests. It took on the work of resuscitating the Children's Sports, previously organised by the Recreational Association, but which had 'fallen by the wayside' possibly because the men were involved in the Armed Forces or other war work.

The Co-ordinating Committee also organised an annual film show for the children for many years, but in the main acted as a watch dog for the area, pushing for better and safer roads and following up on anything that was causing concern to local residents. It was also instrumental in starting up the HORTICULTURAL SOCIETY in 1953 and the fact that the inaugural meeting arranged for 13th February had to be abandoned due to an electricty failure, did not stop the Horticultural Society from going from strength to strength.

Sadly, however, due to lack of support and willingness of people to take on the key roles of chairman, secretary and treasurer, the Co-ordinating Committee was wound up on the 4th of November, 1991.

However, the many and varied organisations continue to grow, with the loss of some and the advent of others. One thing is certain, there is absolutely no excuse for any Blackhall resident to be bored!

CHAPTER 11

THE WAR YEARS

At the start of the 1914-18 War, Blackhall was still a comparatively small village with 350 houses and a population of around 1,500, thus the loss of forty four of their young men must have been keenly felt.

The Congregational News of the period gives some insight into life in the village. In November 1914, the minister, Cecil T. Thornton exhorted the congregation to prayer, faith, action and liberality. The Guild Work Party and the Blackhall Work Party had joined forces and already gone into action and had sent out the following impressive list of parcels:-

147 articles to Soldiers & Sailors Families Association
114 articles to Belgian Relief
57 articles to Craigleith Military Hospital
54 articles to the Red Cross Society
44 articles to the Royal Army Medical Corps
37 articles to Devonshire House
26 articles to Mine Sweepers
24 articles to the Royal Engineers (Forth Bridge)
22 articles to the 9th Royal Scots
18 articles to the Royal Scots (Glencorse)
17 articles to Davie Street School
21 articles in small parcels.

There was also an indication of what life was like at the front in extracts from a letter from Captain Thomas Lindsay R.A.M.C.

> *"There is plenty of work and I feel sorry for you all at home having such an anxious time. One operates, buries, eats and sleeps and marches, or rather rides, so that one gets very little time to think. I have a beautiful horse, 16 hands high, the property of an Artillery officer who was killed and his horse followed my stretcher bearers home and was handed to me. He follows me about, but is a rather clumsy pet. I think we seem to be wiping the ground with Germany but at what a cost of brave officers and men.*
>
> *I have been doctor, chaplain, gravedigger and burier, in fact everything. I buried ten men in one grave a week ago, and last Sunday at a French farm held a short service with some sick and wounded men. I have been reported missing and killed two or three times."*

In May 1916 the Rev. Cecil Thornton resigned as minister 'to serve his country' and his place was taken by the Rev. D.W. Baird. By this time, the church and community's war effort appears to have be taken very much for granted, with little mention being made of it in the Supplement, apart from little snippets such as the following which appeared in October, 1917.

St. Columba's Girls' Guild

The Girls' Guild are still 'carrying on' the Saturday collecting for wounded soldiers started in the first year of the war. Four girls go round their districts each Saturday morning and collect money, scones, fruit, eggs, or books etc. Then they meet in the Church Hall at 2.20 pm. and pack the goods in a basket ready to go down to the two hospitals - Victoria and Flora Stevenson's. The money received is divided - the greater part is spent in cigarettes, and scones are bought with the remainder. During the past year two girls Miss M. Gibson and Miss G Dodds have continued to go down to the hospitals to distribute the goods. Great praise is due to these girls who have gone to the hospitals so regularly every Saturday - wet or fine to do their bit in cheering our wounded.

We are grateful to all those in the village who have given us donations of any kind during the last session and hope that they may continue to give their support to this good work.'

However, there were men too, who remained in the village for one reason or another and **Douglas Fraser** gave this report of them in the Blackhall Bulletin of 1984:-

The Volunteers

The Volunteers - not many readers will remember what might be called Grandad's Army - the Blackhall Volunteers formed during the 1914-18 War from men too old and boys too young to be called up. Unlike the Home Guard in the last war, they were not primarily intended to guard against invasion, as there was no such threat in those days. They were presumably a reserve of man-power to be used if the need arose. One feels that if the German High Command had seen this photograph of Blackhall's keen and determined veterans, they might have surrendered sooner.

In the magazine "The Rec" published at the time, there are various references to the Volunteers, including the following verses taken from a poem by Mr. W.D. Hogg, the editor:

> Now that the war drum's beat is loud and long,
> Behold our Volunteers, some forty strong,
> Turn out to drill with zeal and ardour fired,
> And deem three hours' parade a short sweet song!
> They say those volunteers have come to stay,
> And that they'll get their uniforms some day!
> And rumour says they are a smart platoon,
> And (breathe it not) they'll soon get double pay!

It is interesting to learn that they apparantly received pay, though whether it was just the King's shilling is not known. It seems they were still awaiting their uniform when the poem was written; on the other hand, in another part of the magazine the question is posed: "Why were out gallant volunteers more willing to part with their rifles than with their service boots? Had spade work anything to do with it?" This is a reference to the popularity of allotments at the time, but it suggests that uniforms were about to be handed in.

Mr. Fraser also has some personal memories of the war:-

I can remember the Zeppelins coming over during the first war - my dad got us all up and we all sat under the dining room table. Of course, they dropped bombs on Edinburgh around the Grassmarket. There was a munitions factory in Craigleith Quarry.

And **Miss B Duncan** also has a memory of bombs dropping on Edinburgh:

In the 1914 war, I can remember my mother talking to one of the neighbours and saying "Wasn't that terrible thunder and lightning we had last night" and she said "Oh, Mrs. Duncan, don't be silly that was bombs being dropped at the Castle." And my mother had got into an awful state because my grannie stayed in Grindlay Street, which is just beside the Castle - but by good luck, the windaes were blown in but nobody was hurt.

The allotments mentioned in the Bulletin article were in Gardiner Road, stretching from the main road to what is now Jeffrey Avenue. There were 50 plots, 25 on either side of the main path. The annual rent was 10/-. and a water rate of 1/-. was charged.
Miss Georgie Dodds recalls:-

They were started sometime early in the 1914 war, but I'm not sure whether it was 15 or 16. My father was a keen gardener and over a four year period won six First Awards, four Second Awards and six Third Awards at the Annual Exhibition of Allotment Produce. All the entries in the exhibiton were sold by auction and the money given to the Red Cross.

(Blackhall Bulletin 1981).

It is in the February 1919 issue of the Congregational News that the names of the forty four Blackhall men who were lost in action are listed, along with their rank and regiment, some fifteen of them coming from the Royal Scots, and three being airman and one a naval officer.

The years between the wars were not easy, but Blackhall continued to expand, despite the fact that there did not seem to be much surplus cash around. Many of our residents have memories of the Second World War.

I can remember the day the Second War broke out, there was an alarm at eleven o'clock in the morning. In the house we had in Queen's Avenue, there was a sitting room and what was the living room and what was a scullery in those days. Then we had another small room downstairs in which we used to play with toys and that became a mini air-raid shelter during the war. I remember filling sacks up with earth out of the garden and putting them against the window and we had a cupola which had a blind on it, which we never used but my mother reckoned that it had been put there during the First Work War. And when the war started we had for a short time some kind of blackout curtains, then we got plywood boards put on the downstairs windows. And we must have had a painter in to paint a sort of black border round the cupola between the edge of it and this blind that you pulled over and that did during the war, provided we never put on the top landing light. I think the bedrooms just had blackout curtains. I have a piece of shrapnel about an inch long that was taken off the roof of our house by somebody that was doing slating just after the war - it would be out of an anti-aircraft gun. I remember the two nights of hearing the planes going over to Clydebank, but there was no bombing near here. My mother died in 1943 and the doctor said to me that her death had been hastened by the fact that both the boys were overseas. She wasn't a strong woman and was worrying. Ian was out in India in the Indian Civil Service, and Alastair was actually landing on Sicily on the day she died, he'd been in North Africa. So I'm afraid the war was not a happy time at all for us.

MISS M. MACDONALD

During the war, the army was over at Davidson's Mains and they used to have a battery and the guns used to run up and down, when there was a air raid on.

We were out at Daniel Stewart's and we used to go to school on a Saturday which we didn't like. I was evacuated for a short time at the beginning of the war to North Berwick to my aunt - I was there for about a year. But when we came back - Mary Erskine's and Daniel Stewart's were together and some of Watson's as well.

ANON

My brother and sister were at Blackhall School during the war, they had no school for a while and then they had classes in Miss Aitken's house and various other houses in the district. A lot of the children were evacuated to Alva, we wanted to go but mother said no. We were very envious, we thought this would be great but looking back on it I'm very glad we didn't go. They weren't long away.....maybe a year and then I think the schools started back again so they would come back again.

MISS E. DENHOLM

I came to live in Blackhall in 1939 - we were either going to No 52 Columba Road which was £675 or here which was £650. We were only in the house from the April to the September, when we were evacuated to Bonnyrigg for the war. But bombs were dropped in the Forth and shrapnel fell three gardens along from where John, my nephew, was lying in his pram at Bonnyrigg. So everybody just came home - we came in the January and started to live here and just put up with the war. We had our windows all criss-crossed with tape or something.

At school we used to take the older children to concerts in the Usher Hall, that was something they got during the war. We made the best of things during the war conditions, we did what we could to make it a happy school and not worry about war conditions.

MISS J. WRIGHT

I went to Davidson's Mains First Aid Post, that was my bit of war work at the beginning. When the siren went there was somebody opposite about my age and we used to trek out to Davidson Mains together. Before war broke out my husband was the officer in the local A.F.S., then during the war he was in a reserved occupation but later joined the R.A.F. as an accountant.

A.C.

The Auxillary Fire Service

The Auxilliary Fire Service - a number of Blackhall and Davidson's Mains volunteers joined the Service before the War started and were mobilised in Davidson's Mains School on War being declared. However, it was soon found that there was no immediate need for their services and they returned to their homes. They continued to meet regularly in the old Blackhall School, where they maintained the equipment and took part in exercises such as in the above photograph by the Almond at Cramond.

At the start Mr. Cunningham was the officer in charge, but he went into the

R.A.F. and the late Mr. Ferguson, the Blackhall chemist became patrol officer and carried out his duties with great enthusiasm. We met once a week and we were all prepared to turn out if the sirens went and we had our own pump and vans and so on. Sometimes we went down to Cramond to practise - we had lectures at our meetings and maintained the equipment and so on, and learned how to do fireman's lift etc.

After some time the National Fire Service was formed with full time recruits, but local volunteers, mostly men in reserved occupations, continued to meet in Blackhall until the end of hostilities.

MR. D. FRASER

The Home Guard

We had to meet once a week for drill and a talk and so on. We met on a Friday night and we were allowed to go down to the Edinburgh Academy Shooting Range in Henderson Row. The Academy Sergeant Major was there to give coaching if it was wanted and, of course, he was a first class shot. Shooting, in those days, had a much higher place than it has to-day - I mean if you're a member of a Corps or something like that, you do shooting, but there was an awful lot of shooting went on privately, which I suppose wasn't right. They went to a place in Edinburgh called the Hunters' Bog and they did some practice there, that was away on the other side of the town.

DR. J. HARLAND

The Home Guard - some of the authentic Dad's Army - members of the Davidson's Mains Section of the Home Guard which began as the Local Defence Volunteers hastily created after Dunkirk to assist in repelling the threatened German invasion. Although our local section was based at Davidson's Mains it included many Blackhall citizens and it comprised of quite a large body of men divided up into several units. Parades took place once a week at Davidson's Mains Church Hall and exercises were carried out in the nearby Public Park. Rifles and other equipment were stored in the Church Hall. Although fortunately our part-time warriors were never required to go into action, there is no doubt they could have acquitted themselves well and proved the value of their training.

MR. D.J. FRASER
(Blackhall Bulletin 1984)

The Home Guard on Parade

Another, much younger 'Home Guard' was on duty in Marishal Place.

The flat below ours at 9 Marischal Place was occupied by Mr. & Mrs. Mackay and their family Sadie, Mary and Tom. Tom was a few years older than me and apart from being leader of our "gang" was a great pal. Early in the war, when German paratroopers were hourly expected to descend upon us, Tom organised our stairhead defence. This consisted of (and I can only think that our respective mothers must have been out at the time) suspending various lethal objects by short lengths of string from the bannister rails on the top landing. These included hammers, knives, scissors and our sitting room pouffe. The intention being that when the unsuspecting German Fallshimjagers came charging up our stair, we would cut the string and rain death and destruction upon them. On reflection I don't know about the hammers, knives and scissors, but I am pretty certain our old red pouffe would have accounted for one or two of them.

MR. W. DENHOLM

However, according to St. Columba's Parish Supplements of the period, life seemed to be going on very much as usual in Blackhall. In December 1940, the congregation was informed that an Air Raid Shelter had been provided in the under-building of the church. Access to the shelter could be obtained 'by the door behind the brick baffle wall near the outside steps leading to the minister's vestry.' The shelter was intended mainly for the Sunday School children and a limited number of adults. There was seating accommodation for about 50 people and electric light had been installed. An emergency exit leading to the rear of the church under the new gallery had also been provided.

A later issue gave the practical information that should an air raid alert be sounded about the time of the Service, then the postponed Service would commence a quarter of an hour after the "All Clear", providing this was sounded within the normal time of the duration of the service.

In 1942 the following notice appeared:

EMPIRE SOCIETIES' WAR HOSPITALITY COMMITTEE

Many service men arriving from overseas wish to spend their first leave in our city, and to find that atmosphere of home which is so precious to the exile. An opportunity to provide hospitality in private homes presents itself, and any offers of help in this connection will be appreciated by the Committee.

Bill Denholm writing in the Blackhall Bulletin in 1992 gave an example of 'Blackhall hospitality' during the war.

I have a strong memory of a large convoy of army lorries arriving in the village one Sunday. They drove along Craigcrook Road to what came to be known as "the army lorry field", in front of 'Stevie's Quarry about where the present Blackhall School now stands. The drivers having delivered their vehicles, were probably told that there were no facilities for them at the field, but that they could go down to the village and get a cup of tea there. (in Blackhall on a Sunday?). Soon Craigcrook Place and Keith Row were echoing to the sound of army boots as the soldiers arrived eagerly looking around for a cafe.

Gradually the truth dawned on them and their hopes faded. The cafe was closed. Apart from themselves the village appeared deserted, the window returned blank stares, the doors of the houses were shut fast.

For the troops it was a moment of despair but for Blackhall it was much more than that. Was the village going to fail its fighting men in their hour of need; and most of them Englishmen by the sound of it? Was the village going to fail itself? Not as long as Mrs. Shepherd had anything to do with it. Not by a long chalk! Out she bustled from No 2 Craigcrook Place, a welcoming smile on her face, eyes twinkling behind her spectacles. "Right, you four chaps come in for a cup of tea".

And me at our front window, "Mum, Mrs. Shepherd's just taken in four of the soldiers!" "Right, down you go Billy and bring a couple of them up here". And the doors and windows began to open and neighbours came out into the street, "Come in," and in they came. And as they ate their bacon and eggs and bread and marge, they talked

about their homes and mothers, their wives and children to other mothers, wives and
children. And the fathers talked to them about their experiences in an earlier war and
the soldiers felt they were appreciated after all and wasn't Scottish hospitality great.
And the honour of Blackhall was saved and the villagers acted as they knew they always
wanted to act and felt proud.

There were many ways in which the people of Blackhall helped the war effort. Some were fun like the Spitfire concerts, others were mundane like doing the darning for a nearby regiment or organising refuse collection of vegetable swill for the pigs. All through the war, the Woman's Guild sent out innumerable parcels to various quarters, but in 1943 some extra special parcels were sent out to 186 Blackhall folks who were serving both at home and abroad. The snippets from the letters sent in response show how much they were appreciated and are perhaps summed up in the example below:

It was a very pleasant surprise indeed to receive the registered envelope the other day,
especially to find it was from Blackhall.

First of all please convey to the senders my best thanks for the Postal Order and
the good wishes sent with it, not forgetting the booklet either. Let me congratulate you
though on the photograph of the church. To send it was a happy thought and one very
much appreciated when one is so far from home. It is a fine reminder of the happier
days we once enjoyed, and which we hope will return again in the not too distant
future.

Two years were to pass before peace was declared and these hopes were to be realised, but **Bill Denholm** gives a good word picture of the joy with which V.E. Day was celebrated in Blackhall.

It was mainly we children who went out into the main street and did silly things
without being told to stop. The highlight of the evening was a gigantic and ever
increasing Conga line which snaked backwards and forwards across the main road,
into and out of Ware's Yard, the Road House carpark and finally, the climax, in
through the side door of the Road House, round the Cocktail Bar, into the Main Bar
and out through the front door again. It was exhilarating stuff. Somewhere up ahead
there was a bright new future.

CHAPTER 12

THE GARDEN SUBURB

And what of Blackhall to-day? The sprawling suburb is a far cry from the small village. Has it become too big? Has it lost the strong community spirit which was so evident in the past? It would seem not.

There have been many changes in Blackhall over the past thirty to forty years, quite apart from the many new houses which have been built. Most noticeably has been the great increase in the amount of traffic, causing both noise and air pollution, as well as endangering lives. However successful community efforts have achieved the pedestrian crossing plus traffic islands and the provision of 'lollipop' men or women to ensure the safety of the children.

Another notable change has been the closure of many old and familiar shops - all of them stimulating many memories for older residents. The Buttercup Dairy plus the dairies of McAnsh and Simpson; Buchanan & Calder, Mathewson the Chemist, West the Butcher, Mrs. Hogg the Greengrocer, Scott Lyon and Martins. The list is almost endless but perhaps the greatest 'miss' was the closure of the **Co-op** which had served the community for over fifty years.

Baillie Advertising who took over the old co-operative building

In a 1983 issue of the Blackhall Bulletin, **Martin Browne** gave a potted history of the Co-op

> *In its heyday, the Blackhall Co-op stretched from Craigleith Station to Maidencraig Crescent and sold a variety of goods and services. The building was not erected until the 1920s and the branch opened in 1928 under the grand name of the Blackhall Emporium and contained an impressive list of departments - grocery, butcher meat, drapery, tailoring, millinery, dressmaking, furniture, furnishings, jewellery, upholstery, boot & shoe and drugs.*
>
> *The Blackhall Shop remained largely unaltered until 1943 when most of the departments were closed leaving only the grocery, drugs and butcher meat. This was probably due to the war which hit the association badly with 314 employees being called up. Vehicles were requisitioned and the association forced to spend £14,000 on air raid precautions for its shops.*
>
> *By 1945 the shop was no longer called the Blackhall Emporium and now became four individual shops. In 1948 the butcher meat department moved to 160 Queensferry Road and in 1950 a bakery branch opened at no.186 with a fruit department in no.161. In 1957 Nos 160 and 161 were demolished and made way for the new Maidencraig Court and in 1958 the shop underwent a major transformation which saw all the shops coming under the roof of the present building. There was another major organisation in 1964 when the grocery, bakery and fruit departments were merged into 184-186, but the fleshing department remained at 190, but had to share its premises with the drugs department. The last major reorganisation was in 1968 when the fleshing and drug departments were merged into the new supermarket at nos 184-186 Queensferry Road and is the shop we know to-day.*

Many of our older residents have memories of the Co-op.

> *The Co-op - Oh it was very much in vogue, my mother shopped there and you had a red store book and everything just got written down in it and I thought as a small child that you didn't pay for your messages, that you just took the book. My mother once got a fright, I apparently wandered away from Hillview Terrace when I was two and a half or three and had gone to the store by myself. She was up to high doh and went looking for me and she met me being brought back on the shoulders of this tall grocer from the store - I can picture him still. There was another man in the grocery department called Bob, I've no idea what his other name was, but when you went to a counter to be served - there was no self service then - anyway this man had the most ornate flourishes for writing, he went up and down about six times on the page before he actually wrote anything in your book. As well as all the counters, there was the counting house, where you got the tokens for your milk and where you paid your book at the end of the month.*
>
> MRS. M. EDINGTON

> *The Co-op was a busy, busy shop and it was sad to see the demise of the place. One of the big attraction in the thirties of St. Cuthbert's was the dividend - for working class families the dividend was worth having in those days - it was a real windfall for some of them.*
>
> MR. R. BOYCE

I remember the the Co-op being built when I was a child. My mother went to the Co-op a lot and used to take me when I was of an age too young to go anywhere on my own. It had haberdashery and wool and shoes and things like that. I can visualise it with lots of counters.

MISS M. MACDONALD

And the Co-op used to be really big - Mr. Scott, who was the manager there, said to my sister one day 'there's a hundred pegs in there for the workers to hang their clothes on'. It really was a very good store, the only thing you had to go to town for was clothes other than jumpers and things like than, but you could get everything up there.

MISS E. DENHOLM.

Some familiar landmarks have disappeared completely, such as the old Blackhall School building and the corner of shops pictured below. And in their place the community now has a new large Sainsbury supermarket which helps to compensate for the loss of the Co-op and other shops.

The shops at the corner of Groathill and Craigleith Road

In 1992, changes in the Electoral boundaries did away with the old Telford/Blackhall division and once more split Blackhall in two with part falling into Cramond/Parkgrove and part into Drylaw/Muirhouse. Ravelston and Blinkbonny had already been transferred to Murrayfield/Dean. Protests were made at this decision and **Douglas Fraser** penned his in verse for the Blackhall Bulletin

BLACKHALLICS ANONYMOUS

From the powers that be comes a solemn decree:
There's now no such place as - it started with B
But we can't say the name. It has ceased to exist.
Part Drylaw, part Cramond, it will not be missed.

But we who have lived many years in the place
Will never submit to such foolish disgrace,
From Kirk and from Clubs, shops, households and all
There comes the defiant unanimous call
"Let Councillors hearken, Blackhall is Blackhall!"

The Blackhall Bulletin came into being in September 1980, when St. Columba's Church decided it should make an outreach to the community - and the community, in return, has supported the venture well both in advertising revenue and in contributing news items. One look at its columns shows that the community spirit is still very much alive, with new organisations appearing to replace those which have served their purpose and gone.

Other signs of an active community have been the great support given to recent money raising charity events; the neighbourhood watch schemes which now cover the area; the School Board fighting for more space for the children of Blackhall School and the fact that Blackhall Sports Day continues to be an important event on the local calendar.

But there's an old saying which states 'that the proof of the pudding is in the eating of it', do people enjoy living in Blackhall? The answer seems to be an empathic 'yes', regardless of age, as these items from the children at Blackhall School in 1991 show.

I feel very lucky living in Blackhall. There is so much going on in such a little place. There is a good library with lots of books for young and old. There is a huge park where we can play and have sports days. There are a lot of things going on at the church from Guides and Scouts to a badminton club. The community are friendly and helpful. We are lucky to have a small school set in such lovely surroundings, and although it is on the edge of the city centre, we see squirrels and rabbits that come down from Corstorphine woods. I can't think of anywhere else where I'd rather live

REBECCA SHADE P6

My favourite place is just down the hill from me, where there is a field with about four horses in it. I used to go down there and watch the horses and give them carrots. I enjoy living in Blackhall.

SUZANNE MAILE P7

I like it here in Blackhall
I have lived here since I was small
Most of my friends live here too
Just over the hill from Edinburgh Zoo.

I play tennis quite a lot
I play it more when it is hot
Blackhall Tennis Club is the club I play in
But the games I don't usually win.

The only thing I don't like are the roads
The great big lorries and the massive loads
Outside the School is a lollipop man
And our postman is called Tam.

AMY LAURIE P6

There is a village in Edinburgh,
It's name is Blackhall.
You can bowl all you want
And in the park play football

You can climb up Corstorphine hill, in between the trees,
You can sledge there in winter, when snow covers all the leaves,
You can play on all three tennis courts and beat all your friends
You can run and jump at the sports day, winning gold after the final bend.

MATTHEW ANGUS P6

Similar sentiments were also expressed by members of the **Over Sixties Club**, when in 1991 it celebrated 'Thirty Glorious Years' by having a party and singsong, but new words were put to some on the old songs.

1) There's a village in the town, in the town,
Where Lothian buses set you down, set you down.
Just hold on tight to save the lurch
When buses stop at Blackhall Church.

(Chorus) But it's great to live in Blackhall,
And the reason's clear to all....
But remember do not let the secret fall, fall, fall.
It's me and you, and you and me, and me and you.
I'm glad I'm living near to you, near to you.
If I'm in trouble you're a ready friend....
And for you I'll always backward bend.

2) D'ye ken ony airt as crouse as Blackha',
Wi' a' its big gairdens and hooses nae sma',
Whaur neebors can clash ower ain ither's wa'
Recoontin' the gossip they telt ye?

(Chorus) For Blackha' ma hame an' A dinna want ither.
A canna bide folks gangin' hither and thither.
Aye jist jalouse they live in a dither
An' canna settle doon beside me!

A cam tae Blackha' mony years lang syne.
There were faithers an' mithers an' weans, just fine.
But noo there's masel but I needna whine
A've got freens rounaboot tae cheer me.

There's the kirk up the road - weel noo there's twa.
A went tae the schule but it's no there at a':
An maist wee shoppies hae lang gane awa',
But A've still ma freens roonaboot me.

It's no that faur tae the shops i' the toon,
But I canna thole the rushin' aroon.
A aye want back tae the quate surroon
O ma ain hoose roun the corner!

3. (Chorus) Oh the centre of Scotland is darling Blackhall.
It's the place that is dearest to us one and all,
For you see it's our home where we most long to be.
It's the village that can boast of a high pedigree.

From its quarries of old came the stone for the town.
Great streets and wide squares did its stone masons crown.
The stone was exported by land and by sea
E'en in Buckingham Palace it's Blackhall you see.

Grey Craigcrook Castle protected our land
From English marauders and bold brigand band.
Once the home of Lord Jeffrey, of Constable and Croall,
Its mortification still helps the poor roll.

Even street names recall famous folk who lived here,
The Keith Mar-i-schals and the Strachans, quite near.
By Ravelston's old tower stands the girl's famous school,
With sports and with lessons the days are crammed full!

The farms round the village in name exist still,
Craigcrook, House o' Hill, Maidencraig and Groathill.
For corn crops you now get trees, flowers, hedge and lawn,
But happily you can still hear the bird song at dawn.

It seems there is something in the Blackhall air, that inspires poets of all generations, but perhaps we should leave the last word with the young of Blackhall

Blackhall is the best
Better than all the rest.
Blackhall's where I live
It's where my home is.

I live across the road from the park,
Where you can hear the dogs bark.
Out of my window you can see the trees,
And the footballers with their dirty knees.

We've got a shop,
That sells lollipops
And a school
That's fun as a rule.

Blackhall is the place to be
My friends and I would all agree.

ALISON FORREST P6 (1991)
BLACKHALL PRIMARY SCHOOL

BIBLIOGRAPHY

Census Returns 1841-1891

Craigcrook Estate Records

"The Estate of Ravelston"

Cassels "Old & New Edinburgh"

"Stones & Curiosities of Edinburgh & Neighbourhood"
by George A. Fothergill

"Building Stones of Edinburgh" Edited by A.A. McMillan
(Published by Edinburgh Geographical Society)

Blackhall School Log Books

St. Columba's Church Records

Blackhall United Free Church Brochure

Blackhall Co-ordinating Committee Records

"Memorials of His Time" Henry Cockburn

Edinburgh & Leith Post Office Directories

Old Maps of Edinburgh

General Register of Sasines

INDEX

Adamson, Wm — 10
Aitken, Miss J — 79-80
Alyncrum, John de — 10
Anderson, Sergeant A. — 87
Art Club — 112
Auxiliary Fire Service — 122-123
Badminton Club — 111
Baird, Rev D. W. — 68,98
Berry, Miss, Preparatory School — 76
Blackhall Athletic Lads — 8, 110
Blackhall Library — 108
Blackhall Orchestra — 111
Blackhall Primary School — 76-86
Blackhall Sports Day — 95-97
Blance, Rev R.S.C. — 74-75
Boland, T & Co. — 9
Bonnie Blackha' — 54-57
Bowling Club — 106
Boys Brigade — 67, 71, 99-100
Buchanan & Calder — 20, 87, 127
Burns, Mr. Robert — 24
Chalmers, Mr. McGregor — 65-66
Church Choir — 111
Co-ordinating Committee — 116-117
Constable, Archibald — 11
Craft Group — 116
Craigcrook Estate — 10-16
Craigcrook Farm — 10, 30-34
Craigleith Quarry — 21-23
Craigleith Station — 58-61
Cramond Free Church — 93
Cramond Parish Church — 43, 63-65
Croall, Douglas — 12, 15
Croall, James — 12
Croall, Robert — 12
Cunningham, Mr — 99
Dean Farm — 39-40
Dean Free Church — 63, 93
Dean Parish Church — 63
Denholm Family — 92-94
Denholm, Mr A.S. — 93, 106
Dewar, Lieut, A. C. — 17
Douglas, Rev A. — 73
Dramatic Club — 111-112

Drylaw Estate — 16-17
Duncan, Mr. T — 53-54
Ferguson, Mr. J — 123
Flower Club — 116
Forbes, Robert — 107-108
Foulis, George — 5
Foulis, Sir John — 1, 6
Free St. Stephen's Church — 63
Girl Guides — 104
Girl's Guild — 119
Girls' Work Party — 103
Grassroots — 105
Groathill Farm — 1, 39
Gunn, Mr David — 30
Home Guard — 123-124
Horticultural Society — 116
House o' Hill Halt — 57
Hunter, John — 12
Jeffrey, Lord — 12
Junior Choir — 97, 99
Keith, Alexander — 6
Kerr, Mr. A. C. — 72
Knitting Circle — 116
Lamb, Thomas — 19-20
Leper, Patrick & John — 10
Lindsay, Captain T. — 118
Lothian Chemical Company — 22
Magazine House — 23-25
Maidencraig Farm — 36-38
Maidencraig Quarry — 23-25
Marle Pits — 26-29
Martyrs & St. John's Church — 73-74
Mathers, Miss Preparatory School — 76
Matheson, Rev James — 70-71
Mathewson, Rev. R.J.W. — 72
McAnsh Dairy — 34, 127
Men's Group — 113-115
Merriweather, Rev A — 73-75
More, Sir William — 5
Mother & Toddler — 116
Murray-Gartshore Hall — 6, 43, 63, 77, 106
Murray-Gartshore, Colonel — 6
Murray-Gartshore, Miss — 5, 6-7, 63, 94
Murray, Patrick Keith — 6

Nairne, Baroness	6
Nesbit, Mr George	90-91, 108
Nightingale, Mrs.	13
Over Sixties Club	112
Penny Savings Bank	108
Playgroup	116
Primrose, Sir Archibald	6
Probus Clubs	115
Pryde's Dairy	36
Queen's Court Retirement Homes	86
Ramsay, Wm	16
Ramsay-Gibson-Maitland, Sir James	16
Ravelston Estate	4-9
Ravelston Golf Club	108-109
Ravelston House	4-6
Ravelston Park	95, 110
Ravelston Quarries	19-21
Ravelston Rovers	111
Recreational Association	106-108
Sangster, Rev E.G.	72-73
Scott, Sir Walter	6, 12
Scott, Mr W.M.	89-90
Scottish Country Dance Club	112
Scottish Women's Rural Institute	116
Scouts, The	17, 100-103
Sim, Rev. F.	68-70
Simpson, Mr J.C.	34, 56, 92
Simpson's Dairy	17, 34-36, 127
Snadden, Rev. A.M.	68-69
St. Columba's Church	62-73
St. Cuthbert's Co-operative Society	127-129
Steel-Maitland, Sir Arthur	17
Stevenson, Rev W.B.	64-67
Stewart-Clark, Mrs J.	7, 8
Strachan, Mr. J.	10-11
Sunday School	97-98
Sutherland, Dr.	87
Teenan, Alexander	54
Tennis Club	109-110
Thornton, Rev C.T.	67
Tuesday Topics	116
United Free Church	73-75
Urquhart, Lilias T.,	77
Volunteers, The	119-120
Watson, P/C	88-89
Woman's Guild	115
Young Men's Guild	93, 113
Youth Fellowship	104-105